CA$H CRAFT

The Musings & Meditations
of an Income Investor

DISCLAIMER

This book contains explanations, descriptions, and opinions about investment strategies which may not be suitable for the reader. The author and publisher make no representations or warranties with respect to the accuracy and appropriateness of its content (including material derived from internet sources that may change subsequent to publication) and specifically disclaim any implied or perceived warranty. The book is intended for informational purposes only and should not be considered as investment advice or a recommendation of any particular security, strategy, or investment product. References to specific securities are for illustrative purposes only and should not be interpreted as recommendations to purchase or sell such securities. PhantaSea Books does not endorse the ideas discussed by the author and bears no responsibility for decisions those ideas may influence. Investing entails risk, including the loss of principal, and both publisher and author remind all readers to employ common sense, due diligence, and the insights of licensed financial professionals before undertaking investment decisions.

Dedication

To the Money Muses, past and present; to my father, who first encouraged me to "get in the game;" and to the blessings of patience, perseverance, and an open mind.

CA$H CRAFT. Copyright 2021 by Rancroft Beachley. All rights reserved. No part of this book may be reproduced or transmitted in any manner, electronic or mechanical, including photocopying, recording, or by any information storage and retrieval system, without authorized permission except in the case of brief quotations embodied in critical articles and reviews.

Neither the publisher nor the author assumes any responsibility for changes that occur to referenced websites or data after publication. Further, the publisher does not have any control over and does not assume any responsibility for third-party websites or their content. The book is sold with the understanding that the publisher is not engaged in rendering legal, accounting, or other professional service.

Book design by NeonMind Media, Los Angeles, CA

Cash craft: the musings and meditations of an income investor/ Rancroft Beachley

1. Self-help. 2. Personal Finance

ISBN-13: 978-0-578-74935-8

Published by PhantaSea Books

Honolulu, HI

CONTENTS

Foreword	1
Introduction	5
On Fragility	9
On Risk Awareness	29
On Financial Abundance	51
On Designing the Income Portfolio	65
On Achieving the Million Dollar Portfolio	101
On Promoting the Sex Appeal of Dividends	119
On Investing Beyond the Crossover Point	123
On Non-Numeric Measures of Net Worth	139
On Savings as the Foundation of Wealth	151
Afterword: Income Investing As a Philosophical Approach to Money	167

Foreword

(An Editor's Note, By S. Jacques Stratton)

Wealth merely represents cash flow subjected to the catalyst of time and good money habits.

When the author of this memorable phrase asked me to edit the manuscript draft of *Cash Craft*, I expressed hesitation. An English teacher by trade and an adventure traveler by passion, I feel more akin to the rugged poet than the stock savant. I questioned my ability to offer meaningful commentary on income investing or the good money habits likely possessed by the author and his investment club colleagues. Unperturbed, the author took my doubt as a sign of integrity and offered the reassurance that despite my lack sophisticated financial awareness, I probably had valuable life experiences relevant to the subject matter, insofar as they made me want to improve my relationship with money.

Well, if you put it that way...

Like many Americans whose teenage years coincided with the heyday of shopping malls, I gained access to the working world through the greasy portal of a fast food establishment. I won't use the word "restaurant," as it would only misrepresent, in euphemistic terms, what amounted to a tawdry burger shack. For the grand sum of $3.35 an hour, I helped maintain both the operation's culinary components and infrastructure, cleaning tables, sweeping floors, and traipsing trash. In this capacity, mired in sweaty servitude, I experienced the nihilistic frustration that comes from trading hours for dollars. The frustration turned bitter when Christine K., a high school classmate for whom I nurtured a well-advertised crush, feigned ignorance of our acquaintance, disdaining me and my greasy greeting as she arrived for a snack with her status-conscious friends. My teenage spirit, ever hopeful amid hopelessness, found in these travails a silver lining. If I could only save a sizeable chunk of my earnings, I might salvage a thread of dignity from the tattered fabric of my ego. With enough savings—a teenage version of F-U money—I could quit the burger stand, hopefully in a moment of teen triumph that, I fantasized, might endear me to Christine K., if not her stuck-up friends.

For all its unpleasantry, the burger stand did impart an important life lesson. The frustration of trading hours for dollars prompted me to think critically about spending habits and the chief liability that drained my funds: my '68 T-bird. A prime specimen of the heavy-metal mojo that once characterized American car culture, the beast had an unquenchable thirst for gas and an affinity for the repair shop, traits that an objective cost-benefit analysis identified as busters to a balance sheet. Either I had to ditch the car or work longer hours, a devil's bargain that my teenage heart found highly discouraging. In sum, the burger stand confronted me with one of money's fundamental truths: savings requires sacrifice. Eventually, I quit the burger stand, but I never quit the savings mentality it helped instill.

"Your desire for F-U money helped you perceive cash as an asset," Rancroft told me, musing upon my burger stand experience. "It's an important first step on the path to money maturity."

I figured that counted for something.

Though doubting my subject matter expertise, I offered editorial opinions about the manuscript, which at times took unnecessary detours through monetary minutia. Mindful to the perils of publishing, and with a few minor publication credits to my name, I considered myself attuned to the preferences of today's point-and-click audience, whose appetite for catchy slogans and clever sound bites often relegates more thoughtful writing to the dust bin.

"Some passages need simplification," I said delicately. "Today's reader expects visual cues like bullet points."

"OK, add some bullet points," Rancroft said.

"Also, we need some pictorial enhancements. Most investment books include charts and graphs."

"OK, sprinkle in some charts and graphs."

"Finally, we should omit discussions about obscure ideas. Readers of investing books want wealth secrets, not tangents on the topic of permanent capital equivalence."

At this Rancroft glowered, forearms flexing. Evidently, I'd spoken ill of a sacred subject, and I thought he might punch me in the nose.

"The concept of permanent capital equivalence ranks as one of the most important ideas in income investing," he declared with vehemence. Then, more conciliatory, he advised me not to obsess over reader interest. "Most people don't have a clue about income investing," he confided. "It's highly unlikely anyone will actually buy the book."

"Well, then why did you write it?" I asked, loath to put time into a project that few would appreciate.

To this he merely offered a shrug. "I'm a *rentier* with a six-figure passive income" he said. "I can do what I want."

Well if you put it that way...

Total return, total return
For a positive outcome do I yearn!
One day I'll take a fabulous vacation
But I fret about market fluctuation
A major problem tempers my mirth:
My withdrawal rate depends on net worth!
When markets rise, on a fine nest egg I sit
When markets crash, I'm in really deep sh_t
Yeah, most years my strategy works fine
(as long as I forget about 2009)
But when stocks crash and my stomach upends
I envy those who live off dividends

Introduction

If you could arrange life on your terms, how would you spend your time?

The question invokes philosophy as much as finance, requiring both a qualitative assessment of personal values and a quantitative measure of money. Additionally, the question invites us to ponder the philosophy *of* finance—the purpose of wealth, the proper asset allocation, the ideal investment strategy. This book reflects my attempt to explore these questions according to the "cash craft" mindset advocated by a Los Angeles investment club with whom I associated during the decade spanning 2008-2018 and whose philosophy contributed greatly to my own wealth-building success.

Self-made millionaires representing a variety of professional backgrounds, the investment club hailed from across the greater Los Angeles geographic area. They ranged from middle-aged career-achievers to active retirees, expressed social views that spanned the political spectrum, and followed lifestyles as divergent as that of a pensioner who doted on his grandchildren to a jetsetter whose international travels included adventures in international romance. Once a month, the club met aboard a sailboat docked at Marina Del Rey. From there, as the afternoon sea breeze ruffled the waters of Santa Monica Bay, the group typically embarked on a pleasant day-sailing adventure, taking turns at the helm, indulging a penchant for fine wine, and discussing the theory and practice of their unifying passion: income investing.

The club members referred to their approach as "cash craft" to highlight an income-oriented focus that prioritized cash flow over capital gain. In a world where the mavens of finance preach "modern portfolio theory" and "safe withdrawal rates," the investment club adhered to, and succeeded with, yield-driven strategies that most financial planners consider highly unorthodox. In 2008, when I began attending club meetings, I naively considered myself an informed investor, with over fifteen years' experience investing through bull and bear markets. My familiarity with investment products ranged from plain vanilla mutual funds to options contracts. The ability of my club mentors to confidently achieve success during even the dark days of the 2008-2009 credit crisis, when professional managers succumbed to panic selling amid doubts over the integrity of the financial system, convinced me I had much to learn. Influenced by the club, I tested and eventually embraced their principles in both my portfolio and personal life. Over a decade later, I remain a dedicated disciple of their ideas, and for good reason: income investing provided the cornerstone of a financial plan that enabled me to enjoy a *rentier* lifestyle at an age when most people stress over freeway commutes and office politics.

I don't intend this book as a get-rich guide or how-to manual. Bookstores offer an abundance of such products and I see no need to contribute to the clamor. I have no certification as a financial advisor and construe no part of this book as "advice." Frankly, much of what I present contradicts or at least criticizes mainstream financial dogma. Readers interested primarily in discovering a "wealth system" or "millionaire secrets" will likely find disappointment with a work undertaken as an introspective examination of my own approach to income investing, an investment style, I recognize from the outset, that resonates with a quite limited target audience. The substantial capital required to make an income portfolio viable renders income investing a theoretical concern for most people. The reader likely to benefit most from the meditations presented herein already possesses assets and an inclination to self-manage a portfolio. He or she doesn't need a how-to manual, but rather craves, as I do, writing that examines the philosophy underlying investment choices.

Apropos to the introspective nature of this inquiry, I envision a target audience that resembles me at age forty: established career, salary approaching six-figures, with a brokerage balance around

$500,000. Reflecting on the benefit of income investing in my own life, I think this audience, easily seduced by "leanFIRE" dreams that thwart a chance at real money momentum, stands to gain the most from Cash Craft philosophy. At age forty, I had no idea that within seven years my net worth would double into the seven-figure realm. If these meditations prod an investor in the mold of my younger self toward similar results, I consider them worthwhile.

The reader should regard these meditations as self-contained discussions rather than building blocks arranged toward a cohesive narrative. Relating broadly to the topic of income investing, they touch on a diverse range of discussion points, including

- the "income vs. total return" debate and its implications for retirement planning
- the perception of risk, and the complexity behind the risk/reward spectrum
- income portfolio design styles and the types of holdings they emphasize
- the importance of the million-dollar portfolio, and the savings hurdles necessary to achieve early retirement in a reasonable time frame
- the concept of permanent capital equivalence
- the money habits necessary to grow a dividend stream into a dividend snowball
- the perception of cash as an asset
- wealth metrics that go beyond traditional balance sheet calculations

As creative undertaking and finished product, the book owes its development to several influential voices. For their collective insight about the theory and practice of income investing, I wish to thank my investment club mentors, particularly Clifton, Ruben, Charles, and Bill, whose memorable personalities, commentary, and sincere encouragement proved transformative to my life. I humbly hope this book does credit to their legacy. For feedback on the early drafts of the book, and their assessment of the subject matter's niche value, I wish to thank my colleagues of the Los Angeles chapter of the Society for Technical Communication (STC). Finally, I wish to thank my friend and fellow graduate school alum S. Jacques Stratton, whose editing perspective helped unburden the text of finance techno-speak. His wordsmithing catalyzed the revision process, clarifying the main idea in otherwise tedious passages, and making more readable the occasionally esoteric subject matter.

--Rancroft Beachley,
Los Angeles, CA

--One--

A Meditation on Fragility

> *Written in 2019, ten years into a bull market run that put a spotlight on the price component of the total return equation, the following meditation offers retirement planners a simple perspective: income is more stable than price.*

Prelude: A Conversation between Don and Vinnie

Vin: "Don! Nice to see you back on the links! Are you o.k.? You seem so distracted lately."

Don: "It's the market. It keeps going up and down, flinging my net worth around like a yo-yo."

Vin: "I thought you had everything planned. Didn't you say you were set to retire?"

Don: "That was last week. This week the numbers don't work out so well."

Vin: "What changed your view?"

Don: "I've been browsing the internet, reading popular financial blogs. The bloggers make me second-guess my plans. But I think with enough money and a safe withdrawal rate I'll be o.k."

Vin: "Safe withdrawal rate? What's that?"

Don: "You mean you've been retired all these years and you don't know about SWRs?"

Vin: "I'm a landlord, not an index-fund investor. I own one asset—an apartment building that I bought for one million dollars. I collect rent, and the rent funds my retirement."

Don: "You need to start reading more about modern financial planning! If you did, you'd realize that when you collect rent, you are making a withdrawal."

Vin: "I am? What am I withdrawing from?"

Don: "Well, according to mainstream financial wisdom, you are withdrawing from the building. More precisely, you are withdrawing from the building's 'total return.'"

Vin: "Isn't that an Arnold Schwarzenegger movie?"

Don: "it's not a movie. It's a basic financial concept. Frankly, I don't see how you can retire without understanding total return."

Vin: "I haven't had a problem. Since I bought the building, I've collected a consistent monthly rent of 6K per month. . .that's enough for my greens fees and a new set of clubs every now and then!"

Don: "Whew! I'm glad we talked before it's too late. Collecting 72K/year on a million-dollar portfolio means you have a withdrawal rate of 7.2%. That's risky!"

Vin: "Risky? Says who?"

Don: "The folks who follow the 4% rule, that's who. They could point you in the direction of some respectable retirement withdrawal studies."

Vin: "What should I do?"

Don: "Start learning about total return, and the relationship between income and value. For example, you need to realize that every time you collect rent, you reduce your building's value by an equivalent amount."

Vin: "Really? The real estate broker didn't disclose that."

Don: "It's true, nevertheless. And if an exchange priced the building in real time, like stocks, the exchange would have to lower the price every time your tenants mailed you checks."

Vin: "Gosh. . .I wish I had learned about this sooner."

Don: *"And that's not all you need to worry about. You also need to consider the impact of price volatility. Think about what happened during the recession. Your million-dollar building was worth only 500K."*

Vin: *"Really? I had no idea."*

Don: *"Didn't you follow the news? The whole country was in crisis!"*

Vin: *"My rent kept coming in, so I didn't worry about prices."*

Don: *"Didn't worry about prices! My friend, you absolutely have to worry about prices!"*

Vin: *"I figured as long as the income remained stable, prices didn't matter. And that's how it's worked out."*

Don: *"You've been lucky, my friend. . .very lucky."*

☙❧

Though portrayed as caricature, our friends Don and Vinnie reflect common financial planning issues that confront investors as they approach retirement. Despite the stability of income relative to price, the income approach remains a curiosity among financial advisers, whose preference for mainstream financial dogma perpetuates "drawdown phase" planning assumptions. Unfortunately, in the financial arena, where the human psychology of fear and greed both drives the system and comprises its fundamental weakness, shocks inevitably disrupt market-dependent designs. The institutional embrace of sophisticated products like credit-default swaps, combined with the speculative financing encouraged by low interest rates, multiplies scenarios where illness in one market sector leads to contagion throughout. Inevitably, through repeated crises, the fragility of the system forces investors to confront the fragility of their own financial philosophy.

Following the publication of Nassim Nicholas Taleb's *Antifragile*, a book which explores how systems weaken or improve as a result of disruption, fragility and finance increasingly appear together as keywords in economic discussions. Questing for an anti-fragile future, retirement bloggers attempt to insulate their lives from disruptive financial events. The strategies proposed—multiple streams of income, side hustles, vegetable gardens, off-the-grid lifestyles, stockpiles of cash, gold, or even ammunition—reflect memories of financial crisis and its lingering trauma. Other writers relate fragility to financial shame, exposing in a confessional manner how their lives exemplify the face of America's new economy, where even well-educated, accomplished professionals live one disruption away from disaster. We hear of former jetsetters reduced to living in cars or the basements of friends, and one-time management moguls now working retail. Behind the voyeuristic appeal of these confessions lies an argument with overtones of social justice—a system must be wrong if it brings fragility to the lives of people who do things right.

Amid such stories, writing about the fragility of millionaire retirees seems indelicate. People think of the "retirement crisis" as a problem of Americans too economically stressed to build their 401Ks, not a problem of the leisure class with portfolios extending into seven figures. Unfortunately, decades of traditional financial advice, advocating "drawdown phase" management strategies, brings fragility into the finances of people not normally considered fragile.

The Fragility of Price-Based Calculations

The early retirement community devotes enormous attention to backward-looking simulations which extrapolate future returns from past data. The resulting advice—safe withdrawal rates, net worth minimums, model asset allocations, rebalancing protocols—drapes an illusion of certainty over an intrinsically uncertain situation. Prisoners of the present, prospective retirees rely on the past to glimpse the future. In practice, this means plugging portfolio value into a "Monte Carlo" simulation, a computer calculation that utilizes various inputs to plot a graphic depiction of a portfolio's chances of surviving the retirement decades. Unfortunately, placing price (i.e. portfolio value, an unstable number) at the center of the calculation, the assessment only amplifies an unstable outcome. Running current values through past data gives investors an illusion of control. In reality, they get a portrait of fragility.

The vaunted 4% rule, the F.I.R.E. community's go-to answer to unpleasant questions about uncertain outcomes, represents an eagerly accepted effort to exert control over fragility, promising retirees a safe withdrawal rate likely to provide years of inflation-adjusted stipends. The 4% dogma propagates so widely, and in such an unquestioned manner, that many remain ignorant of the research (published by Bill Bengen in a 1994 issue of *The Journal of Financial Planning* and reexamined by the 1998 "Trinity Study") responsible for the idea. Ignorance of the original research leads to ignorance of the rule's key assumption: that by selling shares, investors realize a total return from a broad allocation to stock and bond indexes. Based on this assumption, the rule presents a price-based portfolio drawdown plan that attempts to balance spending and longevity.

Unfortunately, price-based plans amplify instability rather than protect against it. As such, the 4% rule provides a poor answer to fragility, especially when even its promoters lose faith. The 2008-2009 financial crisis, following closely on the heels of the "dot-com" bust, led many in the financial planning community to declare a "lost decade" for stocks and question the long-term data which provided the basis for the 4% rule. Suddenly, responding to warnings that characterized the 4% rule as too reckless, planners began advocating the "3% rule," advising prospective retirees to keep working until their nest eggs swelled to a number roughly thirty-three times their anticipated annual spending (rather than the previously recommended twenty-five). Interestingly, doubts about the withdrawal rate number didn't raise any questions about the price-based total return ideology behind the calculation.

Widespread acceptance of withdrawal rate "rules" casts a stigma on alternative approaches to retirement planning. Unfortunately, popular thinking can prevent an open-minded consideration of options that, depending on individual situations, might prove more suitable. Observing my investment club mentors derive significant cash flows from income strategies unaffected by market fluctuations, I questioned the prejudice of popular opinion. Where 4% dogma sees a million-dollar portfolio in terms of its 40K initial draw, income investors derive 60K-80K per year without selling shares. When asked by skeptics about risks inherent in yield-based investment approaches, the investment club offered a succinct rebuttal: *income is more stable than price.*

The Income Alternative

Income investing opens the door to price-agnostic retirement planning. For the fragility-conscious retiree, this represents a paradigm shift with implications for portfolio management. Total-return approaches, dependent on random price movement, place portfolios at the mercy of market speculators. Income strategies, by

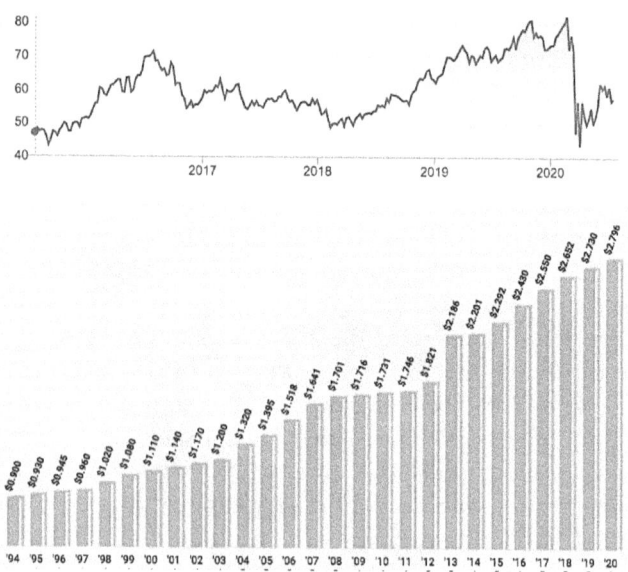

"Income is more stable than price:" two views of Realty Income Corporation, one depicting five years of price swings (top), and the other depicting twenty-five years of steady dividend growth (bottom). Upon what metric would you design a retirement plan? (Chart data courtesy Google Finance and Realty Income.)

contrast, produce results from predictable cash flows. Where modern portfolio theory encourages investors to hedge volatility, diluting capital in broad market indexes that mix both quality and poorly performing enterprises, income strategies maximize the quality/productivity balance. Income, a more stable number than price, allows investors to extrapolate reliable expectations from prior results, creating a sense of control unavailable to total-return investors. Despite these benefits, income investing remains a curiosity of the financial world, largely because of biases which collectively emphasize price-based thinking—biases which not only marginalize income strategies, but lure retirees toward fragile futures.

Mainstream Financial Biases

Media coverage of investing tilts heavily toward a price-based focus. Most news stations summarize the day's financial developments through snapshots of major market averages, with "up" days applauded by green arrows and "down" days mourned by red—a myopic practice, especially in the context of time frames that offer a critique of price-based metrics. Over the thirteen years from 1999-2012, for example, the S&P index provided a price-based return of 0.4%. However, the result improved dramatically when measured by income. Investors who collected and reinvested S&P dividends achieved a 26.3% return over the same period[*]. During the 2008-2009 crisis, headlines dramatized the magnitude of market swoons, yet glossed over a significant phenomenon:

---

[*] Jim Jubak, *Juggling with Knives*, (Perseus Books, 2016). A widely followed finance writer, Jubak deserves honorable mention for recognizing the vulnerability of the financial system even before the market implosion brought on by the 2008-09 credit crunch. Though not a dedicated income investor, Jubak writes frequently on matters relating to income investing principles, and I recommend his voluminous work to interested readers.

excluding the financial sector, most dividend-paying corporations maintained or even increased dividends.

Unfortunately, the media's mainstream target audience—people whose investing priorities center on their 401K balances—remains receptive to the myopic focus on price. Inevitably, this results in a widespread and persistent public attitude that views gains as positive and declines as negative, an attitude with psychological implications for fragility. Up-market trends turn the gears of greed, resulting in FOMO—fear of missing out. Traders feel inclined to employ increasingly risky strategies, such as buying stocks on margin, to juice gains. During the inevitable sell-off, "FOMO" reduces to simply fear. If the sell-off turns severe, fund managers, anticipating redemption orders or margin calls, sell indiscriminately. The "weak hands"—buyers arriving late with little reserve and an interest in speculative gain—sell whatever they can to raise cash. Dramatic headlines trumpet the declines, and the cycle continues, feeding fragility.

Income investors lament the price-centric coverage of financial news media, noting that an emphasis on price obscures other important data, such as the consistency of dividends. They especially critique the media's tendency to portray upward price moves as positive and downward moves as troubling. Echoing Warren Buffet's famous dictum to "be fearful when others are greedy," they regard upside moves as the real danger. Built on greed, upside moves implicitly bring more risk into the market.

Rather than promote euphoria over up-market days, the media might better serve the public by creating excitement about dividend boosts, a more reliable indicator than share price of corporate health. Income-focused reporting, highlighting cash flows that accrue regularly to shareholders regardless of price, would help instill confidence in the fearful and quell the voices of cynics who view investing as another form of gambling. Income investors don't gamble; they derive results not from random price movement but predictable cash flows. Unfortunately, stability makes boring headlines.

If the media disdains income investing for its lack of drama, the financial industry disdains its simplicity. A strategy dedicated to the passive collection of dividends, interest, and distributions requires little professional advice. The mutual fund industry, built around fee-laden products and expert management teams, benefits from portraying investing as a complex procedure beyond the skillset of the average person. The message: only in partnership with professionals can someone outperform markets and achieve retirement goals. Income investing threatens this paradigm, since income investors have no need to outperform. Rather, they measure success by a simple metric: whether income covers living expenses.

Additionally, the temperament of the investing public helps contribute to the marginalized status of income investing. People harbor a psychological preference for optimistic outcomes. The long-term upward trend of the stock market instills an optimism bias that finds excitement in "sexy" growth stories. Income investors, with their drab stories of digging for dividends, discover they make uninspiring cocktail party conversation. Rumors about the next tech IPO that promises quick capital gains generate more attention than the stalwart dividend history of electric utilities. As a mind state with psychological and social benefits, optimism deserves cultivation. As the basis of an investing strategy, optimism paints rosy hues over an uncertain premise: that one can buy smart and sell smarter, relying on "greater fools" to bid up prices. To the optimistically minded, strategies which prioritize income over capital gain cast doubt on that premise, representing a cynical effort to hit singles rather than a glorious pursuit of home runs.

The Income vs. Total Return Debate

Mainstream finance, through its tendency to marginalize income investing, sets up a false dichotomy, portraying income investors as inhabitants of a universe separate from the one inhabited by seekers of total return. An investment for income still generates a "total return," albeit one derived primarily from the income portion of the total return equation. Both approaches entail risks subject to criticism. Income investors deride total returners for "chasing growth" and, in exchange, garner accusations of "chasing yield." For the early retiree in possession of a million-dollar portfolio, seeking cash to fund real-life expenses (for illustration, suppose an initial 40K per year), the debate reduces to a simple question: what strategy more reliably promises an inflation-adjusted 40K? An income plan paying 50K (5% yield on a million dollars), or a "withdrawal rate" plan that derives 20K from income and 20K from selling shares? With the first option, income exceeds expenses, allowing for a reinvestment of the difference, producing a higher income total the following year. With the second plan, expenses exceed income, forcing the investor to sell shares to make up the difference. Accordingly, an answer to the above question requires us to consider the consequence of selling shares.

Case Study: A Lesson in Productive Potential

To what extent does selling shares confront the retiree with fragility? Ultimately, this issue centers the debate between income and total return. Richard, a sailing aficionado who occasionally accompanied the investment club on sailboat excursions, found the matter particularly troubling. A veteran of the advertising industry, he considered himself savvy to promotional schemes, and thought he recognized a bit of propaganda in investment club principles that made income investing seem a magical solution to retirement planning. Since share-selling underlay his retirement plans, he had difficulty keeping an open mind toward the club's criticism of the practice and wondered why withdrawal-rate fragility applied to him but not income investors.

Answering, the investment club offered a unique perspective: income investors, they posited, occupy the same position as landlords collecting rent or farmers collecting a harvest. Since neither rent collection nor crop harvesting reduces the *productive potential* of the underlying enterprise, withdrawal rate metrics don't apply. Put another way, the intrinsic worth of the enterprise, measured by the net present value of future anticipated cash flows, remains unchanged.

Aware of Richard's skepticism, they challenged him to find a financial planner who would tell landlords or farmers that successful management of an apartment building or a farm required compliance with the 4% rule. On what premise would a planner give such advice? Relishing his chance to point out an inconvenient observation, Richard mentioned that most portfolios don't typically hold apartment buildings or farms. Richard thought he scored a point, until my investment club colleagues informed him that they owned plenty of rental real estate indirectly through REITs, and enjoyed the profits of farmland via preferred stock of an agricultural co-op.

Elaborating further, club members offered an interesting critique of the 4% rule. The research that provided the basis for safe withdrawal rates, they observed, considered only broad market indexes, and thus glossed over (or ignored) specific security types, such as REITs, preferred stock, MLPs, specialty finance, specific segments of the bond market, and specific dividend-oriented segments of the stock market. In other words, the research didn't carefully examine the range of securities to which income investors gravitate.

Discomfited, Richard returned to his wine, while my club colleagues repeated their idea that in the investing world, "withdrawal," properly defined, describes share-selling that reduces productive potential.

On this matter, the income vs. total return debate reaches new levels of animosity, inspiring disagreement about even the definition of terms. Rarely do the advocates of one philosophy change their opponents' minds. Still, with overtones of Hamlet, the fundamental question lingers: "to sell or not to sell?" By way of answer, income investors highlight the idea that spending investment income, much like collecting rent, incurs no corrosive effect on a portfolio's productive potential. The future anticipated cash flow remains unchanged.

Share Selling and Sequence Risk

Selling shares to fund cash payouts incurs a subtle but over the long term significantly corrosive effect. If the share-selling involves income assets, such as the bond portion of a traditional portfolio, the future income dwindles. If the selling comes from "growth," i.e. the equity portion of a traditional portfolio, then the handicap of a reduced asset base limits future gains. Share-selling precipitates more share-selling, a negative cycle that eventually depletes a portfolio. An up-market year might conceal the corrosion, giving the retiree temporary confidence that down-markets tear away. Withdrawing, on December 31st, 40K from a million-dollar portfolio that returned five percent for the year leaves the retiree 10K in the green ($1,050,000 − 40K= $1,010,000). If the million-dollar portfolio suffered a five percent loss, the same withdrawal leaves the investor 90K in the red ($950,000 - 40K= $910,000). Another loss in year two—an additional 5% perhaps—intensifies the decline, especially after factoring in that year's inflation adjustment. Market gains in year three could provide improvement, but the now-depleted asset base requires a Herculean effort to restore the portfolio near its earlier glory. This scenario, illustrating sequence risk, leads financial planners to label the span encompassing the five years before and after retirement as the "fragile decade," a time frame when a poor sequence of returns significantly impairs an investor's ability to meet retirement goals.

When expenses exceed income, unfavorable moves in share price carry a significant impact. During down years, selling shares to fund withdrawals forces retirees to book losses, which otherwise exist only on paper. With investment income greater than expenses, income investors can afford to regard price declines for what they usually represent—buying opportunities. The "Taper Tantrum" of 2013 provides a prime example. Prices on bonds, preferred stock, and income plays like REITs took a hit, as rumors about the Federal Reserve's plans to end its program of quantitative easing spread through the market. True to the "income is more stable than price" mantra, the cash flows of such securities remained unaffected, and income investors scooped up attractive yields during a sell-off that proved overblown. The Taper Tantrum showed that income investors with confidence in their holdings and a stockpile of cash reserves can afford to view price declines as something to welcome, not something to fear.

The Confidence of Cash Flow

What gives an investor confidence in a portfolio? As with definitions of the term "withdrawal," the answer depends on which strategy—total return or income—the investor advocates. Followers of the 4% rule find confidence in the long term historical trend of markets and from the broad diversification of their market-index holdings, a diversification which leads them to cast a cynical eye at the concentration risk (the emphasis on only a portion of the market) that income investors apparently embrace. Conversely, income investors critique the dilution risk of broad market indexes, noting that ownership of the "market" inevitably allocates funds to troubled ventures with unstable prospects. Uncomfortable with this criticism, advocates of the total return thesis wonder if a tilt toward income really assures a better result. After all, companies can cut dividends, and bonds can default.

A rebuttal of this point merits some elaboration. In my experience, people who raise the specter of dividend cuts typically belong to a cohort of dedicated mutual/index fund investors with very little background managing a portfolio of individual securities, and who consequently have little understanding of the due diligence income investors employ. People afraid of dividend cuts ignore, or conveniently forget, data showing that during most time-frames dividend hikes outnumber cuts by a significant margin. Additionally, their fear foregrounds a perspective of shareholders as helpless victims, adrift among the shoals of corporate finance.

They reference Enron, or General Electric, or some other cherry-picked story of corporate malfeasance to exemplify the contention that today's dividend darling can, without warning, become tomorrow's dividend disaster.

Such stories represent the exception far more than the rule. Apart from the truly "black swan" disruption to global business wrought by the 2020 pandemic, in most circumstances a careful perusal of quarterly earnings, cash flows, and payout ratio trends will help investors sniff out potential problems. An investor exercising proper due diligence in 2007 could unmask GM, burning at that time through billions in cash, as a pension plan that happened to make cars on the side*, and expose GE as a company mired credit troubles thanks to risky lending at its GE Capital finance unit. Seasoned income investors also understand that the inevitable occasional mistake won't blow up portfolio. A stock doesn't go to zero just because a dividend gets cut. A portfolio of fifty equally weighted securities yielding 6% overall would require three of them to lose their entire market capitalization to significantly mar the portfolio's productivity for that year. In truth, for every General Electric, General Motors, or Enron that delivered a setback to income investors, one could identify hundreds of "growth" stocks that disappointed advocates of the total return thesis--and not just during one black swan event, but in any given year.

As for preferred stock and bonds, the rank of these securities in the corporate structure gives them a priority claim on cash flows. An issuer of preferred stock must pay the "coupon" in full before paying a single penny to holders of common shares. (Awareness of this has enabled me to find great investments in the preferred shares of certain companies whose common stock the market views skeptically.) An issuer of bonds, recognizing the punitive

---

* <u>While America Aged</u>, Roger Lowenstein's insightful exposition of America's pension troubles, notes that by 2006 GM existed more for the benefit of the UAW than for shareholders, allocating, over a fifteen-year span, 55 billion to pensions, while paying only 13 billion in dividends.

consequences of default, will strive to meet its obligations in all but the worst circumstances. From a risk standpoint, an allocation to preferred stock and bonds represents an assumption well-supported by historical data—that through the ups and downs of the economic cycle, the underlying issuer won't always thrive, but it will most probably survive.

Putting Risk in Perspective

Though income investors can afford price agnosticism in their portfolios, they face the threat of price pain at the supermarket, the gas pump, or retail shops where rising costs of consumer goods play havoc with household budget forecasts. The investment income that funds a comfortable lifestyle in a 2% or 3% inflation environment may well prove insufficient if inflation doubles.

As of 2019, inflation remains tame, well within its 3% historical rate, and doomsayers (typically gold bugs) extend ever further into the future their prediction for a day of reckoning. My investment club mentors—veterans of the 1970s and 1980s, when inflation soared into double digits—offered sage advice drawn from the perspective of actual experience. Inflation, and its financial market counterpart, interest rates, can behave in one of five ways: go down a lot, go down a little, stay the same, go up a little, or go up a lot. Of these, only the last—inflation and interest rates going up substantially—entails a serious threat. Even then, the threat depends as much on the *speed* of the increase as its amount. A period of slowly rising inflation and interest rates allows investors to adjust, progressively deploying capital toward securities with higher income potential. In a period of rapidly rising inflation and interest rates, however, the inflation spikes outpace the adjustments, and pain precedes equilibrium.

Markets have a way of turning hubris to humility and rendering premature most prognostications. Wise investors, much like military planners, consider both the likelihood of intended outcomes and unforeseen adversity. Sometimes, however, emotional thinking and psychological bias cloud the difference between healthy skepticism and unhealthy paranoia. Living in Southern California, I see this dynamic play out frequently among friends who act blissfully nonchalant about the very real threat of earthquakes yet worry obsessively about what style of garage door best enhances home value. The same ironic logic makes investors flock to unproductive holdings like gold because they fear the one-in-five scenario of sharply higher inflation and interest rates. (Investors interested in thorough economic explanations about why this scenario remains unlikely should consult the quarterly economic outlook reports from Hoisington Capital Management, whose analysts maintain a contrarian lower-for-longer inflation/interest rate thesis borne out by current events.)

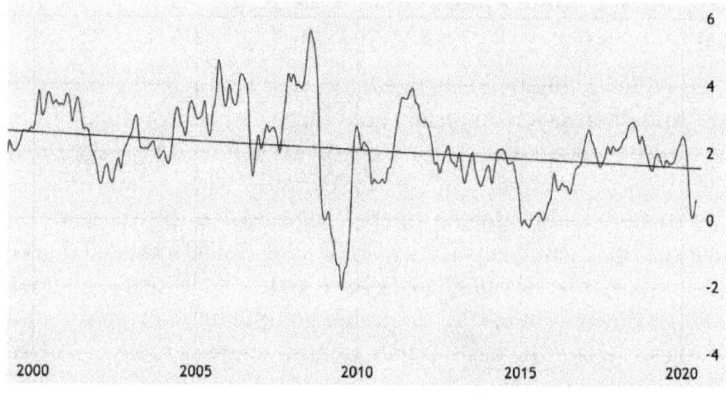

Inflation data spanning the two decades from the Tech Bubble to the Covid Crisis. Does the downward-sloping trendline support a lower-for-longer rate thesis? Note the flirtations with deflation in 2009, 2015, and 2020. (Source: U.S. Dept of Labor)

Intending no insolence to the inflation gods, I offer here an assessment that (hopefully) allays the fears of investors who hesitate to allocate capital to "rate-sensitive" securities. First, the current economy bears little resemblance to the heavily unionized manufacturing economy of the 1970s. Workers today retain comparatively insignificant power to command wage hikes, contributing to the fact that in real terms, today's wages parallel those of forty years ago*. Anemic salaries leave little discretionary income and push only lightly on the inflation levers. Second, demographics increasingly render the first-world economic landscape a domain of retirees. Aging populations don't contribute much to GDP; rather, as economists note when studying the example of Japan, an imbalance between workers and retirees tends to hamper economic growth. Add to this the cost savings of corporate outsourcing, the reduced pricing power of OPEC, plus a likely return to higher unemployment rates, and talk of serious inflation remains a campfire story.

For the sake of thoroughness, let's consider the more plausible scenario of inflation ticking gradually higher, and examine the implications not only for retirees with income-oriented portfolios, but also those pursuing a traditional "drawdown plan." Assume both sets of retirees have million-dollar portfolios from which they hope to fund annual living expenses initially set at $40,000. If, by the second year of retirement, inflation rises by 4% (instead of the historically anticipated 3%), the retirees face a COLA of $1,600, a number $400 greater than anticipated. Viewed another way, the inflation uptick confronts the retirees with unanticipated additional expenses of just over $33 a month in year two, a bit of budget-creep that both sets of retirees may find unpleasant.

The difference manifests in how the retirees "hedge" the situation. The income-oriented retiree cares about protecting the value of a relatively small number—monthly cash flow. The drawdown plan retiree wants to protect a relatively large number—total portfolio value. The income retiree, with cash flow greater than expenses, will redeploy the excess into additional cash flowing investments. Assuming the portfolio produces $50,000 of

---

* Drew Desilver, "For Most U.S. Workers, Real Wages Have Barely Budged in Decades," Pew Research, 8/07/2018. Much of the commentary about financial shame, financial fragility, and other buzzwords referencing the vulnerable state of American workers ties back to the phenomenon of wage stagnation.

investment income, a 5% overall yield on a million dollars, the retiree will have an excess of $10,000. Invested at the portfolio's average yield of 5%, the excess will produce an additional $41 per month in year two, easily covering the budget-creep. By contrast, the drawdown-plan retiree faces a more uncertain task: trying to preserve the real (as opposed to nominal) value of a million-dollar portfolio that a 4% inflation rate threatens to erode by $40,000 in year two. Gold, the traditionally recommended inflation hedge, will likely provide the "answer." Unfortunately, gold provides no cash flow, reducing the portfolio's productive potential. An allocation large enough to make a difference would require the elimination of more beneficial assets (e.g. real estate, commodity-oriented equities, etc.). The result: more share selling.

In practice, the inflation fragility faced by income investors arises less from systemic forces than from personal behavior—in other words, lifestyle creep. Put another way, the fragility of income investing comes not from the difficulties of fitting a budget over a lifestyle, but rather the difficulty of keeping a lifestyle within a budget. Typically, this happens to those who assume too quickly the *rentier* lifestyle without fully understanding the dynamics of *rentier* life. The scenario often proceeds as follows: aged thirty-or-forty-something, tired of cubicles and soul-sucking corporate bosses, the aspiring *rentier*, in possession of a decent six-figure nest egg (say, $400,000-$500,000), relocates to a romantic locale and hoists the banner of work-optional life. Inevitably, the romantic lifestyle entails romantic relationships, often with sly vixens who coyly develop their roles as recipients of largesse. A taste for champagne replaces a taste for beer, expensive outings replace low-cost entertainment, and the budget that once seemed right proves uncomfortably tight. Though conveyed as caricature, variations of this scenario play out with disturbing frequency, and more disturbingly when big-city budgets exert proportionally larger damage on proportionally larger nest eggs.

Properly executed, income investing entails both a financial philosophy and a lifestyle philosophy. Retirees whose lifestyle dependency places them at the high end of income dependency will have a low margin for error and proportionally greater fragility. The transition to retirement doesn't excuse the income investor from retaining at least a portion of the savings mentality that enabled retirement in the first place. As a guiding mantra, "income is more stable than price" provides investment reassurance. A balanced lifestyle helps the retiree keep income higher than costs.

When from growth stocks investors flee
Heed the advice of the sage retiree:
To income securities you must dedicate!
Re-think your concept of safe withdrawal rate!
Though the critics pronounce doom and gloom,
The income portfolio continues to bloom
To this, the critics say tisk-tisk--
Don't you know higher yield means higher risk?

--Two--

A Meditation on Risk Awareness

> *Having attained capital, the investor must deploy it for productive use, an enterprise that entails confrontation with financial market volatility. Written in 2019, the following meditation provides an overview of how income investors assess risk and introduces the psychological and behavioral attributes that facilitate progress toward financial independence. In the process, the meditation argues that risk lies not so much "in the market" as in the mismatch between investor expectation and asset performance.*

Prelude: A Further Conversation between Don and Vinnie

Vin: "Don! Nice to see you back on the links. . .been a while!"

Don: "Yeah, I've just been working a lot. When I do have time off, I haven't been playing much golf."

Vin: "Why not? Are you still worried about the market and what the retirement bloggers say?

Don: "That's right. How did you know?"

Vin: "You have that same worried look as the last time I saw you."

Don: "I suppose I do. Just when I think I have my retirement figured out, the market changes, and then I have to re-calculate my withdrawal numbers."

Vin: "That sounds frustrating."

Don: "How about you? Still chasing skirt in Rio?"

Vin: "Not lately. Some friends have invited me to join them as a partner in a gas pipeline business, and I've been reviewing the income statements."

Don: "Oh? What do the income statements tell you?"

Vin: "Well, based on past cash flows, the business will likely deliver a stable income stream."

Don: "Vin, Vin...it's good you told me about this. You're about to make a big mistake."

Vin: "I am? Says who?"

Don: "Mainstream financial planners, that's who. If you followed their advice, you would know that past performance can't predict future results."

Vin: "Well, my experience shows that cash flows can be stable over time. Consider my apartment building. It's delivered very stable cash flows. And after looking at the income history of this gas pipeline, I'm willing to bet it can deliver stable cash flows as well."

Don: "Vin, no offense, but your experience doesn't prove anything. You mention two cherry-picked examples and think that you've discovered a great investment strategy. Sure, the apartment building and the gas pipeline might perform well for a period of time. But over the long haul, how can you be sure? Yesterday's dividend darling might be tomorrow's dividend disaster. Look what happened to Kinder Morgan, Wells Fargo, or Enron. If people stop living in apartments or using gas, you'll be devastated."

Vin: "I guess you have a point. What do you think I should do?"

Don: "You need to diversify. Your myopic fascination with income exposes you to concentration risk. Instead of owning a segment of the market, you need to own the entire market. You need something called an index fund."

Vin: "Own the entire market? That sounds crazy!"

Don: "Actually, it's the only way to fully diversify and reduce risk."

Vin: "Don, I'm familiar with real estate, and in real estate the mantra is location, location, location. For example, my apartment building stands across the street from a college, which supplies a reliable stream of tenants. If I owned buildings everywhere, I'd have both winners and losers. Why do I want losers?

Don: "Vin, just think what you are saying. You are saying, 'I can pick a winner.' What makes you think you're so great? Do you realize that most professional money managers can't beat the market?"

Vin: "They can't?"

Don: "No. That's one reason for the popularity of index funds. Think about it. . . no need to pick winners. No need to think you're great when you're really not. Just relax. . .and when you need cash, you can still generate income!"

Vin: "I can? With my money spread among winners and losers, how can I get much income?"

Don: "Easy. You can MANUFACTURE dividends by selling shares."

Vin: "Manufacture dividends? Sounds like something Bernie Madoff might do."

Don: "That's because your focus on income makes you ignorant about the role of price as a component of total return. If you paid more attention to price, you'd realize that you can use price increases to your advantage. A dollar of capital gain spends just the same as a dollar of dividends. Why not use the power of price to increase performance?"

Vin: "I don't need price to increase performance."

Don: "Why not, Vin? What makes you so special?"

Vin: "I take Viagra, and it works fine!"

Wealth builders who understand capital's productive use gain a more equitable position in their relationship with money. Yet deploying capital productively often entails exposure to risk.

Income investing, which equates asset worth to the net present value of future anticipated cash flows, offers a unique perspective for the cultivation of risk awareness.

The successful investor seeks assets that maximize the quality/productivity balance for the long term. However, the prospect of buying a security that subsequently declines in price keeps many prospective investors on the sidelines, where they remain hostage to the idea that they will "get in the game" once the market provides a more favorable entry point. Doing so reflects a twofold ignorance: one, perfect entry points appear so only in hindsight, and two, price frequently portrays an inaccurate reflection of value. *Price* summarizes the opinions, ranging from rational to irrational, of buyers and sellers. *Value* summarizes the net present worth of future anticipated cash flows. The assessment of value, independent of price, lays a foundation for more sophisticated risk awareness.

The transition from risk aversion to risk awareness marks a major milestone for the aspiring *rentier*. In Cash Craft philosophy, risk tolerance carries a somewhat different meaning than the one standardized in mainstream finance, where it measures how investors react to unpleasant volatility. For income investors, risk has nothing to do with the possibility that a security purchased for twenty-five dollars today will only catch a bid of twenty dollars tomorrow. Rather, income investors locate risk in the possibility of *unanticipated impairments* to a security's future anticipated cash flows. Accordingly, risk awareness reflects an investor's confidence in the productive potential of his/her portfolio.

This idea highlights a key difference between income investors and mainstream finance. Income investors don't prioritize capital gain. Receiving their returns primarily from income, they regard price volatility as incidental noise, a minor static muted through fine tuning of the dividend dials. By contrast, mainstream finance obsesses over price, believing it a consensus view of worth. In large part this belief stems from the widespread acceptance of the Efficient Market Hypothesis (EMH), which posits that market participants, possessing equal information and profit incentive, exert an equalizing force that eliminates inefficiencies across the risk/return spectrum.

As with many ideas of academic origin, EMH enjoys a theoretical acceptance that sugarcoats its practical shortcomings. Considering the limitations of EMH, well-regarded fund manager Howard Marks writes *"I do not believe the consensus view is necessarily correct. In January 2000, Yahoo sold at $237. In April 2001 it was at $11. Anyone who argues that the market was right both times has his or her head in the clouds; it has to have been wrong on at least one of those occasions"**. Despite its limitations, EMH remains prevalent in mainstream finance, contributing to an index fund ideology dependent on broad market performance, regarded by many as the premier display of efficiency. Income investors derive confidence not from the efficiency of broad markets, but from the stability of income relative to price.

Complexities behind the Risk/Reward Spectrum

The transition from risk aversion to risk awareness requires the aspiring income investor to perceive the complexities that lie behind the risk/reward spectrum. Adjusted for inflation, so-called risk-free financial assets—savings accounts, CDs, money-market accounts, and other products designated as cash-equivalents—rank poorly on the scale of productivity. Investors hold these assets for their quality and stability, not for the expectation of real returns or money momentum. Though traders and fund managers may use the phrase "going to cash" in the course of their operations, cash and its equivalents almost never offer such compelling returns that they merit a large allocation in a portfolio.

---

* Howard Marks, *The Most Important Thing*, (New York: Columbia UP, 2011). While Marks questions the widespread acceptance of EMH, he respects one of its chief implications: that investors rarely gain undue advantage without assuming undue risk, a subject to which he devotes three book chapters. I recommend Marks' book for its insightful commentary, which I think offers value to both experienced and novice investors alike.

I say *almost never* because under certain infrequent circumstances, marked by inverted yield curves and historically tight credit spreads (a condition prevalent just prior to the 2008-09 financial crisis), cash equivalents can make excellent holdings—provided the spread between nominal yield and inflation allows a real return.

While the role of cash in an income portfolio deserves discussion as a subject unto itself, no serious income investor would allocate the bulk of a portfolio to cash. Income investors, both novice and experienced, may periodically increase or decrease their cash reserves, depending on yield metrics like the spread between bank CDs and quality dividend stocks. Generally, however, cash occupies a peripheral place in the income portfolio, for the simple reason that other asset choices offer better potential for long term income stability. Paradoxically, the interest rate dynamics that occasionally make cash an attractive asset occur during peak economic growth, and usually portend recession and a decline in short-term interest rates. (In the wake of the 2008-09 Financial Crisis, a portfolio that remained heavily in cash suffered a major productivity impairment from the Federal Reserve's "ZIRP" policy.)

Risk as a Mismatch between Expectation & Performance

A tendency to equate risk with price volatility only clouds the true nature of investing. The possibility that "safe" (i.e. stable) assets can, over certain time periods, subject an investor to purchasing power loss requires investors to re-think traditionally conceived notions of risk. Similarly, the occasional tendency of "risky" assets to exhibit price behavior unrelated to underlying cash flows raises questions about the reliability of price as a measure of corporate health. In May 2015, shares of Altria traded at $51. Four years later, after significant swings, shares returned to the May 2015 level, despite a quarterly dividend increase of 53% (from .52 to .80 cents). Via dividend hikes, managers of the tobacco giant expressed a different outlook than the one embraced by the market, which fixated on concerns about FDA regulations and lower-than-expected enthusiasm for e-cigarette technology. To reprise Howard Marks' criticism of efficient markets, either the May 2015 or the May 2019 Altria share price indicates market error, since awarding the same bid for substantially different cash flow defies logic.

The example of stock price volatility highlights a key aspect of risk awareness. Risk doesn't exist "out there," waiting to snare investors who venture into the murk of the financial forest. Rather, risk occurs in the mismatch between investor hope and asset performance. The behavior of Altria shares between May 2015 and May 2019 showcases this dynamic. Investors with an expectation of income did well, receiving dividends that grew by 53%. Price agnostic, they derived benefit from Altria's adept management of historical cash flow trends. Meanwhile, market participants interested in chasing Altria's potential growth bore much greater risk, as mixed data regarding smokeless tobacco technology incited price panic. Depending on expectation, the same asset displayed different performance and risk parameters.

Defining risk as a mismatch between expectation and performance applies to not only securities markets but to the psychology of personal finance. People express trepidation toward the stock market, thinking it a risky place for their hard-won savings, yet gladly commit large sums to houses and cars, as if these purchases signify a realm immune to financial risk metrics. If houses and cars carried a listing on the **NYSE**, the **NASDAQ**, or some other exchange capable of tracking real-time liquidity (as measured by a constant reporting of bid-ask spreads), people would have a much different appreciation of the true risk involved. On many days, the house or car of such pride to the owner might not even catch a bid, rendering its true worth a matter of conjecture.

In professional money management circles, securities rendered illiquid by a lack of ready buyers, and whose infrequent trading makes price a matter of subjective estimation, carry designations as "Level Two" or "Level Three" assets for the purpose of risk disclosure. By contrast, most commonly traded market securities carry a less-risky "Level One" rating. I raise the matter not to discourage the purchase of cars and houses (although Richard Marston, in his 2014 book *Investing for a Lifetime*, presents studies that seriously undermine the conventional wisdom of housing as an investment) but to reveal the hypocrisy of commonly held risk perceptions. In both personal finance and securities markets, the savvy investor recognizes the complexity that lies behind the risk/reward spectrum.

The mental outlook that underlies risk awareness requires the wealth builder to recognize the role personal perception plays in the creation of risk. Early success in the investment world can inflate the ego to a point easily ruptured when markets behave badly. Conversely, early disaster can so traumatize investors that they remain blind to future opportunity. Both outcomes produce a similar consequence: a misperception of markets that keeps potential investors sidelined.

Case History: Sideline Regret

Mr. Salesi, the supervising pharmacist of a drugstore where I worked during college, remains indelibly in my mind as an example of sideline regret. One day, when a temporary pharmacist expressed plans to work reduced hours on a freelance basis, Mr. Salesi, with overtones of jealousy, asked how the temp could afford to give up full time employment. In reply, the temporary pharmacist revealed that she had ploughed her earnings into mutual funds. Years of market gains had given her a nest egg that made the rigors of full-time work unnecessary. Asked in turn why he continued to work such long hours, Mr. Salesi donned a sad expression, and recollected a time early in his career when he'd "lost his life savings" to the stock market. Now, he insisted, any attempt to seek returns greater than bank interest rates would only invoke "Salesi's Law," a mystical financial phenomenon applicable specifically to him. Mr. Salesi believed the moment he committed money to the market, "Salesi's Law" would ensure his investments declined at a velocity directly proportional to the hoped-for return.

To me, at the time a young investor making my initial foray into the market, these words carried a chilling overtone that hid their comic quality. Hearing first-hand the account of someone who "lost his life savings" to the stock market and thereafter remained subject to the capricious wrath of the finance gods put a damper on my investing enthusiasm, until I realized that the same market one pharmacist found so fearsome rewarded the other with pleasant returns. I wondered if the former's experience truly reflected investing risk, or instead risk arising from his own idiosyncratic approach.

As it turned out, Mr. Salesi sought the investment equivalent of a "home run," placing the entirety of his capital into a handful of pharma stocks that, based on his inside knowledge of the industry, offered the potential for explosive growth. Unfortunately, opportunity for explosive growth usually comes with the threat of implosive decline, as indeed transpired when the FDA threw a wet blanket of delay over the market's enthusiasm.

Human Error as a Source of Risk

To the prudent income investor, this case history reveals a few crucial money mistakes. The eagerness to "hit a home run" by concentrating capital in micro-cap pharma stocks indicates a personality inclined toward impatience and greed—traits incompatible with the objective evaluation of risk. As a young professional enjoying good income and job stability, Mr. Salesi had no reason to swing for the fences. His investment approach suggests that he entered the market without a reasonable, clear objective for his capital. "Making a lot of money" does not constitute a clear objective. (Over what time frame? In relation to what standard?) By contrast, the risk-aware income investor might seek a different goal: a seven percent annualized return over ten years, sufficient to double one's original capital—a goal well within the parameters of reasonable market returns.

In addition to illustrating the consequence of poor planning, the story highlights the danger of fallacious thinking. The pharmacist

Rate of Return	Years to Double an Investment
3%	24
4%	18
5%	14
6%	12
7%	10
8%	9
9%	8
10%	7

Approximate years required to double an investment per "Rule of 72" (doubling time = 72 divided by rate of return).

erroneously assumed that his expertise as a pharma industry insider would confer expertise in the way financial markets valued pharma stocks. In truth, financial markets often price securities in ways completely unrelated to the business prospects recognized by insiders. While inside information sometimes provides the basis for a compelling investment thesis, any approach lacking proper risk awareness courts failure. Mr. Salesi could have benefitted from John Maynard Keynes famous dictum, "the market can stay irrational longer than you can stay solvent." Ironically, the market did eventually recognize some of Mr. Salesi's picks as winners— just not in a time frame that the pharmacist could tolerate. Psychologically, he failed to grasp the implications of his experience. He blamed his failure on the whimsical mood of the market, rather than the inherent weakness of his own perception. Consequently, he remained ever after on the sidelines, invoking "Salesi's Law" as a crutch for his pessimism.

Through the course of my investing career, I have encountered such case histories in their various permutations—people who "lost their life savings" to the stock market, people whose lifestyles declined when the market swooned, people who derided the market as a form of "gambling" because they bet and lost. On the surface, the stories share a common element—a tendency to portray "the market" as a source of risk while portraying the investor as a helpless victim. Those who subscribe to this view believe that mere chance distinguishes winners from losers. Dig deeper, however, and one finds a tale of human error: concentrating too much capital into one stock or industry, relying too heavily on broker-supplied leverage that resulted in margin calls, employing derivatives strategies with potential to blow up a portfolio, etc.

Marc Allaire, in his insightful book on options trading*, uses a memorable acronym to describe an investor's flirtation with risk. POGWO, or the "possibility of getting wiped out," measures in percentage terms (roughly estimated) the chance a strategy might result in ruin. Assessing POGWO requires the prospective investor to examine both the market's likelihood of accommodating a particular strategy, and, just as importantly, the investor's motivation in pursuing it. In other words, POGWO encourages a sense of risk awareness both internal and external in scope.

Key Traits of Risk Aware Investors

Students of the money game make great progress toward risk awareness when they honestly scrutinize their own psychological temperament. Though a full explication of risk awareness could require a book unto itself, the following traits, annotated with brief explanations, offer a general sense of the temperament typical of risk-aware investors:

♦ *they feel comfortable purchasing a security—stock, bond, mutual fund, etc.— and disregarding, for months at a time, its subsequent price behavior.*

With income investing, only two prices matter: purchase price and sale price (or, in the case of fixed income securities, the redemption or "call" price). Everything in between amounts to unimportant

---

* Marc Allaire, *The Options Strategist: How to Invest and Trade Equity Related Options,* Boston: McGraw Hill, 2003.

static. If the purchase represented the thoughtful outcome of proper due diligence, then it should inspire confidence in what that bid reflects—the net present value of future anticipated cash flows, a metric frequently overlooked in the day-to-day fluctuation of market opinion.

♦ *they feel comfortable with the possibility of sudden and steep market declines*

As a young investor, I steeled my nerves with the advice of a finance professional: *expect a ten percent correction at any time.* In an investing climate still rife with memories of the 1987 market crash, when the Dow lost twenty-five percent over two days, such advice reflected common sense. Through the course of my investing career, this advice has helped me remain nonchalant toward market moves that the media sensationalizes yet history reveals as normal deviations. To put it bluntly: if you can't stand the prospect of the market spilling 100K of red ink over your million-dollar portfolio, then you really shouldn't be in the market at all. The point here involves psychology rather than portfolio management. Just as mountaineering requires climbers to master their fear of heights, so should investors master their fear of volatility. In the end, no hedging technique or allocation strategy can both maximize profits and minimize loss. The best hedge comes not from the market but from confidence in the durability of one's personal financial foundation.

♦ *they feel comfortable "going long" an equity position without the quasi-insurance of put-options or brokerage stop-loss arrangements.*

Income investing recognizes a stock for what it truly represents—an ownership stake in a company. Income investors "go long" an equity position because they want to own the cash flows of the underlying business. Hedging that ownership through artificial gimmicks suggests a lack of faith in one's preliminary due diligence. If you trust the opinions of the market more than your own due diligence, you will achieve only limited progress in the transition to risk awareness.

♦ *they pay attention to yield spreads*

Risk doesn't exist in a vacuum. Astute income investors glean its presence from the way assets perform relative to each other. Cash Craft philosophy regards the junk bond yield spread, measuring enthusiasm for junk bonds relative to ten-year treasuries, as the key metric for evaluating overall market risk. Operating on the premise that high junk bond prices signal the market's heightened disregard of risk, my investment club mentors considered spreads tighter than the historic norm* as a warning sign. Other spread metrics, such as the tax-adjusted yield difference between municipal bonds and treasuries, between bank CDs and the dividend average of the S&P 500, and between the Fed Funds Rate and the long bond, also merit attention. The point: a thorough assessment of risk requires an awareness of bond market dynamics.

♦ *they strive to maximize assets and limit liabilities*

Income investors prioritize cash flow over capital gain, and measure value by extrapolating those cash flows into the future. Accordingly, shrewd *incomistas* allocate capital only to those things for which they can identify a clear cash flow metric, and avoid things like gold, precious stones, bitcoin, fine art, collectibles, etc. which offer no basis for that determination and whose profit potential depends entirely on the willingness of "greater fools" to bid up prices. In the transition to risk awareness, this trait proves key, for it provides a double benefit: not only does it offer a shield

---

* Anette Thau, in her Bond Book, a classic introduction to the fixed income market, considers 400 bps as the normal junk bond yield spread by historic standards. A tighter-than-normal spread (e.g. 300 bps) functions as a warning sign, while a wider spread (e.g. 600 bps) typically signals buying opportunities. Just prior to the 2007-2009 financial crisis, spreads reached an exceedingly narrow 200 bps, a sign of significant underlying risk. In the middle of the crisis, spreads widened dramatically, by some measures more than 1000 bps, an excellent buying opportunity.

from the volatility inherent in the game of greater fools, but it assures that capital goes where needed most—to productive use.

"Crapital Assets"

I list the above trait last because it introduces a primary cause of financial failure: a tendency to acquire liabilities that negate, or significantly counterbalance, the benefit of assets. Having achieved the money milestones of savings, career, and high income, the aspiring wealth builder may feel able to afford indulgences that masquerade as valuable things but, on a balance sheet, prove destructive to wealth. The investment club referred to these as "*crapital* assets," a term rich in ironic tone meant to convey the true nature of the item. Crapital assets include a range of material goods often sought by the newly affluent: boats, motor homes, expensive recreational equipment such as jet skis, jewelry, home décor, etc.

In the list of "crapital" assets, cars rank especially high. A fascination with cars usually correlates negatively to the building of wealth. A house, if owned long enough for a homeowner to build equity, might offer asset potential (for more on the dubious value of housing as an investment, see Chapter 13 of Richard Marsten's *Investing for a Lifetime*) and meanwhile satisfies a basic need for shelter. Cars, by contrast, epitomize the word "liability," something that incurs costs rather than produces income. When people attribute to a car anything more than its function as a personal transportation convenience, and flaunt to fellow commuters the bells and whistles of car culture, in effect adding to the cost of a liability-laden machine, they reveal such a distorted sense of risk in their personal finances as to render suspect their sense of risk in the world of investing. True, the garages of the wealthy may house fancy cars[*]. The already-wealthy can easily

---

[*] Most, however, don't. According to the authors of *Millionaire Next Door*, "some millionaires do spend considerable dollars for luxury autos. But they are in the minority." To indulge in a tangent, I should mention that driving habits, regardless of make and model driven, provide a strong indication of income investing stamina. Aggressive drivers, swerving around fellow commuters in a mad dash

absorb liabilities too burdensome for others. When the aspiring wealthy fail to recognize the true costs behind the facade, they impair their chances to achieve higher-level money milestones.

The cultivation of emotional and mental restraint necessary to avoid liabilities that masquerade as valuable things advances a person far on the road to risk awareness. However, because the dynamics of fear and greed easily sway the human heart, one might possess a cerebral awareness of risk, yet behave emotionally as a speculator, to destructive effect. Probably nowhere does this dynamic sow more confusion than in discussions about the merits of gold. Gold bugs defend the metal as an asset, saying it provides a storehouse of value, serves as a hedge against the politics of fiat currency, and offers safety in times of fear. Cynics counter that gold's "value" arises entirely from its historical and largely irrational grasp on the human psyche. For sage perspective on the subject, we can consult Warren Buffet, the "Oracle of Omaha," whose 2011 Letter to Berkshire Shareholders opines as follows:

> *Today the world's gold stock is about 170,000 metric tons. If all the gold were melded together, it would form a cube of about 68 feet per side (picture it fitting comfortably within a baseball diamond). At $1750 per ounce—gold's price as I write this—its value would be $9.6 trillion. Call this Pile A. Let's create Pile B costing an equal amount. For that, we could buy all U.S. cropland (400 million acres with output of about $200 billion annually), plus 16 Exxon Mobils. . .can you imagine an investor with $9.6 trillion selecting Pile A over Pile B? A century from now the 400 million acres of farmland will have produced staggering amounts of corn, wheat, cotton, and other crops—and will continue to produce that valuable bounty, whatever the currency may be. Exxon Mobil will probably have delivered*

---

for the next red light, reveal a temperament unprepared for a successful transition into risk awareness. Driving dramas that arise from the pressure of a high stress job, high stress relationship, or high stress life signify frustration and a mind-set geared toward emotional decisions.

trillions of dollars in dividends to its owners and will hold assets worth many more trillions. The 170,000 tons of gold will be unchanged in size and still incapable of producing anything. You can fondle the cube, but it will not respond. Admittedly, when people a century from now get fearful, it's likely many will still rush to gold. I'm confident, however, that the $9.6 trillion current valuation of Pile A will compound over the century at a rate far inferior to that achieved by Pile B.

In this missive, Buffet displays a diplomatic tone, seeking a nice way of calling gold bugs what they really are—"speculators." Buffet, quite simply, does not view gold as an investment. It offers no cash flows to evaluate, and no product line of fundamental value to society. In Buffet's philosophy, people who buy gold for profit engage in speculation, not investing. To profit, the buyer of gold depends entirely on the "greater fool theory"—the belief that another buyer will pay an even higher price.

The thought of gold has led people to act with great stupidity since ancient times. The investment club criticized gold's allure, regarding it merely as a product of the metal's psychological association with nobility and wealth, since other than a very limited industrial value, it offers no practical usefulness. It looks pretty, not because of any fundamental quality, but because society conditions us with messages both subtle and overt. We see gold adorning today's glitterati much as it did Cleopatra. In this sense, gold has much in common with high fashion, except a fur coat provides warmth on a cold night.

In short, gold doesn't qualify as an investment because it doesn't provide cash flow. By definition, *an investment is an asset that provides cash flow*, and successful income investing requires the accumulation of cash flowing assets. Though obvious, this statement carries implications worth considering. The standard advice of mainstream finance pushes the budding investor toward a capital gain mindset, driven by a focus on equity growth. Cash Craft philosophy critiques both this mindset and the "accumulation phase" ideology behind it.

The demand for cash flow causes income investors to ignore wide swaths of the market. With regards to equities, this tendency invokes some debate. Meir Statman, in a 1984 article titled "Exploring Investor Preference for Cash Dividends," posits that a dividend bias stems from an illusory distinction between dividends and capital. To Statman, dividends and capital gains derive from the same corporate asset base, so focusing on one over the other amounts to an arbitrary distinction. Income investors, noting substantial differences between dividend and non-dividend equities, critique Statman's view as grossly simplistic. The following rationale provides an overview of income investors' preference for dividends:

♦*Dividends represent real cash, not paper earnings that may reflect creative accounting.* Through the declaration of a dividend, corporate boards recognize the right of shareholders, as owners of the company, to claim their share of cash flows. By contrast, a company that pays no dividend effectively snubs shareholders' intelligence, asserting that management knows the best use for earnings—an assertion called into question by the long history of profligate corporate spending.

♦*A dividend signifies the operational stability of a business strategy.* The premise here relates to efficiency and the generation of free cash flow. A successful company will reach a point where it generates more free cash flow than it can reinvest in its business at an attractive return. A company that can't (or won't) distribute cash to shareholders raises suspicions about the long-term viability of its strategy.

♦*Established in a regular pattern of payments, a dividend creates a market expectation that managers strive to fulfill.* Non-payers, lacking the constraints of such an expectation, often redeploy capital into foolish ventures.

♦*In times of market turmoil, dividends provide a cushion against short sellers, who must add the dividend amount to the cost of selling short.* No such cushion exists for non-dividend equities. During selloffs, short sellers can and do push their prices much lower.

Finally—and in my view, of prime importance—*a dividend provides a clue about a company's long-term return prospects*, something difficult to ascertain with non-dividend equities. To estimate the long-term return of an equity holding, the investment club utilized a back-of-the-napkin version of the Gordon Growth model, extrapolating long-term return from the sum of current yield and dividend growth rate. Accordingly, a stock with a 5% current yield and a 5% average dividend growth rate should offer a 10% long term return. Focusing on long term return keeps the budding investor on track, maintaining an objectivity unimpaired by the distractions of market volatility and speculative ventures.

While cash flow as a guiding principle of security selection tends to concentrate a portfolio into certain market sectors, the benefits of such "concentration risk" often get overlooked. Investing for cash flow maximizes the time value of money, which prioritizes a dollar of dividends today over the possibility of a dollar of capital gain tomorrow. Additionally, it shields the investor from the emotional dynamic of fear and greed that influences price action in all securities but especially dominates the pricing of speculative ventures. Guided by cash flow, the income investor ignores the hype surrounding IPOs, the media sensationalism that enhances market euphoria, and the graphic alchemy of chart technicians, who tout MACD signals, RSI indicators, and other numerical nuances to divine "safe" buy points.

Meanwhile, the income focus nudges the investor toward securities he/she might never consider otherwise. Preferred stocks, for example, rarely receive mention in the media. Financial advisors sneer at them, repeating the cliché that preferreds offer all the risks of stocks and none of the benefit of bonds. The criticism overlooks the fact that preferred stocks enjoy a sizeable interest among institutional investors and pension fund managers. Many real-estate investment trusts issue preferred stock as part of their capital structure. The securities offer exceptional yields and price stability, yet receive very little attention from financial advisors, despite the benefits of such securities to income-needy retirees (Ralph L. Block, in his books and articles on REITs, provides an excellent overview of these securities). PDT, a closed-end fund with a substantial allocation to utility preferreds, boasts a multi-decade income and price history that deserves study by prospective retirees. Over the twenty-one years between 1995 and 2016, PDT, on a per-share basis, fluctuated around an average price of $10.65, offered an average yield of 8.1%, and produced a cumulative income (per share) of $18.26. A million dollars invested in PDT in 1995 produced an average of $81,734 per year in income through 2016, numbers that reveal 4% rule ideology as unnecessarily limited at best.

Resisting "FOMO"

As *rentiers* who achieved great benefit from the theory and practice of income investing, my investment club colleagues understandably voiced a steadfast admonition: investors should demand cash flow from their capital. I use the word "steadfast" to highlight the fact that the club stuck by this principle even when income generating assets significantly underperformed other securities. They voiced it especially when enthusiasm for sexy "growth" stocks or well-hyped IPOs dominated the headlines, viewing such enthusiasm as "growth-chasing"—a sure sign of the FOMO (fear of missing out) typical of speculative bubbles.

Resisting FOMO requires the aspiring *incomista* to exert tremendous discipline. Dedicated pursuit of the strategy (or any strategy, for that matter) will inevitably incur periods of underperformance, which require patience to endure. To delight in dividends, the financial equivalent of mining for copper, while others reap sizeable cap gains (the financial equivalent of striking gold) takes patience and a degree of faith. Regret over missed profit can sometimes nag investors to the point they lose sight of their core strategy. Regret may channel remorse when hedge fund and mutual fund managers dump income assets in order to raise cash

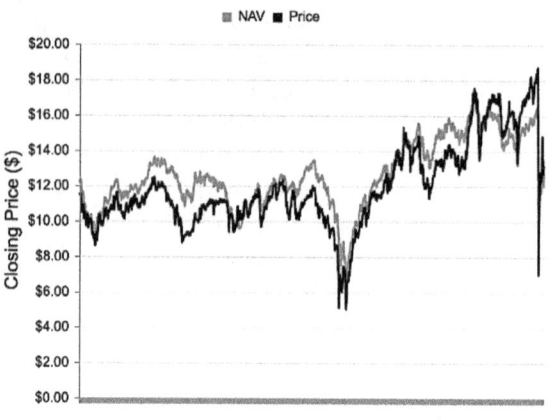

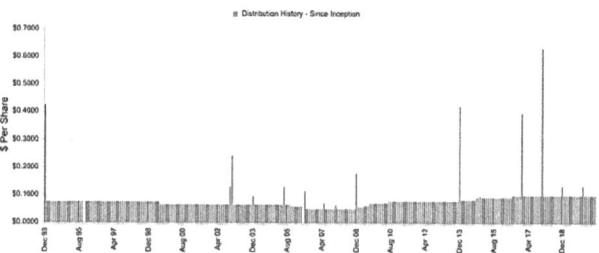

PDT price history (top) and distributions (bottom), mid 1990s-2020 (source: CEF Connect). With dividends reinvested, a 10K investment grew over five-fold during this time—not bad for a fund concentrated heavily in utility preferred stocks.

necessary for growth-chasing. Those of us who remember the market action just prior to the dot-com bust, when fund managers voiced the mantra of "this time it's different" and ditched their stalwart holdings to load up on dot-com darlings whose prices bore no correlation to earnings, know that good investments sometimes get no respect* Interestingly, for income investors who stuck to their guns, the frenzy of the dot-com bubble offered a perfect opportunity to load up on long-term treasury bonds—at the time, one of the most un-loved investments around.

Risk Awareness and Money Momentum

To the students of the money game I offer some advice of my own: income investing starts as a sweaty marathon, but over time turns into an effortless glide. During the initial phase, the results accrue slowly—like coins in a jar—a dividend here, a fund distribution there. Years may come when the growth-chasing sprinters pass by in a blur and boast of big returns to cocktail party audiences that ignore the income-seeker's copper mining success. Let the sprinters boast. Typically, their outsized gains turn to outsized losses when markets turn south. Meanwhile, income investors benefit from a stream of dividends and interest that brokerage statements always report as a positive number.

Ultimately, successful risk awareness results in a robust and growing stream of investment income. Where the early stages of money maturity encourage a delight in savings, the later stages encourage a delight in dividends. As with the psychology of savings, the psychology of dividends gains power when founded on a pleasurable vision of the future. Measuring monthly investment income as a percentage of monthly living expenses can help anchor this vision. A person with expenses of 3K per month might chart investment income in $300 increments: the first ten percent of monthly expenses, the second ten percent, etc. Such a metric offers

---

* Howard Marks, in *The Most Important Thing*, regards occasional underperformance as a requisite for success. "Since many of the best investors stick most strongly to their approach—and since no approach will work all the time—the best investors can have some of the greatest periods of underperformance...see Warren Buffet in 1999. That year, underperformance was a badge of courage because it denoted a refusal to participate in the tech bubble."

a mental guidepost that encourages perseverance in the quest to contain expenses and grow income.

To this end, the investor should gain confidence from the knowledge that, over time, the combination of investment income and savings act like wing-shoes, accelerating the aspiring *rentier* through the later portions of the money marathon. The attainment of successive income increments occurs with increasing rapidity. The last increment bears a special designation: The Crossover Point, where investment income exceeds expenses. Passing it, the investor discovers new levels of money momentum, and enjoys the vistas reserved for those who approach the doorstep of a work-optional life.

--Three--

A Meditation on Financial Abundance

> *Written in 2018, this meditation references statistics supplied by the 2017 Credit Suisse global Wealth Report. Though the data may change, the basic principles still apply.*

A clever vocabulary, promoted by lifestyle coaches and finance gurus, now pervades the internet. Where past generations offered the unpleasant yet effective admonition that riches require hard work and savings, today's money muses invite their audience to "win the money game" by "shifting frequencies." If we accept the metaphor their vocabulary promotes, we can believe that wealth, like sunshine, radiates with widespread resplendence; we need only adopt an "abundance mindset" to enjoy it.

If seekers of wealth needed only a proper money mind to achieve their goal, the world would abound in millionaires. Instead, less than 1% of the world's population controls assets of one million or greater. 95% of the world's adults, and 75% of U.S. households, never achieve wealth greater than $350,000. In their eagerness to promote the money mind, today's finance gurus rarely discuss the Pecuniary Paradox: in a world of abundant wealth, there remains a scarcity of wealthy.

The word "abundance" implies a grandeur that affects us emotionally. We imagine money in such quantities that it functions like the air, flowing through our bank accounts the way breath flows through our lungs, independent of conscious effort on our own. As an income investor whose assets produce significant monthly cash flow, I admit the comparison has merit. However, even though my dividends roll in automatically, I remain conscious of my spending, knowing the role budget-mindedness played in enabling me to attain HNW (high net-worth) status.

I suspect most self-made millionaires can attest to the depiction of millionaires in *The Millionaire Next Door*—those who amass wealth as a result of hard work, saving, and disciplined investing remember well the balance-sheet mentality of their pre-millionaire days. The biographies of the bankrupt abound with stories of people who went from riches to rags because they spent without thinking, racking up expenses higher than income, trading long term wealth for short term pleasure. When we consider that seventy percent of rich families lose their wealth by the second generation*, the use of the phrase "financial abundance" represents a marketing gimmick, referencing a lifestyle that sounds fantastic but reflects values antithetical to the long-term preservation of wealth.

Yet if the word "abundance" over-reaches in its implications, it nevertheless provides a useful reference, denoting a state of wealth much greater than that suggested by mere "sufficiency." On the spectrum of retirement lifestyles, it occupies a place well opposite that of "leanFIRE," the designation of financial freedom in its most basic form, where wealth generates income sufficient for life's bare necessities —food, shelter, inexpensive hobbies, and perhaps an occasional social indulgence.

---

*Catey Hill, "Here's Why 90% of Rich People Squander Their Fortunes," *CBS Marketwatch*, April 23, 2017. Hill cites a study by the Williams Group that finds 70% of rich families lose their wealth by the second generation and 90% by the third generation. The statistic offers a reflection of the way people confuse riches for wealth, and indicates that wealth mindsets do not arise automatically from proximity to money but instead require cultivation.

Abundance and Time Freedom

To the extent that leanFIRE defines a retirement lifestyle according to *needs*, abundance, we can infer, defines a lifestyle according to *wants*. The inference leads to a corollary worth consideration. A lifestyle based on the satisfaction of wants must first possess a key attribute: time freedom. In turn, time freedom implies that income derives from assets rather than labor. The investment portfolio functions like a money machine, making dollars and channeling them to an owner/operator, who may on occasion monitor its productivity, yet remain blissfully detached from the details of its daily management. Financial abundance, thus construed, confounds the marketing rhetoric of internet money mavens. Their advice to "shift frequencies" applies not to the *rentier*, passively collecting cash flow from investments, but rather to the laborer, for whom the phrase functions as a coded message: "work smarter."

Like most glittering generalities, the message dangles a psychological lure, attracting those eager to associate with smartness. The sophisticated wealth builder, however, prefers to "receive" money as a *rentier* than "earn" money as a laborer, for whom the exchange of hours for dollars inevitably results in the sacrifice of something irreplaceable (time) for something mundane (money). Here a question naturally arises: can a career, even a well-paying one, can count as an asset?

Strictly speaking, assets produce *passive* income for their owners. Common examples from the investment arena include dividend-paying stocks, preferred stock, real estate investment trusts (REITs), actively managed closed-end funds, MLPs, etc.— investments that produce "unearned" income for which the IRS allows a preferential tax treatment. To obtain this income, the owner need not contribute the slightest bit of labor, time, or skill. Careers, by contrast, produce "earned" income—compensation for services—taxed at increasingly onerous marginal rates. No perquisite can varnish an unpleasant truth: a career, even one considered highly lucrative, remains at essence a glorified means of trading hours for dollars. Of course, the careerist might critique this assessment as an oversimplification. Careers provide both remuneration and important psychological benefits, including social connections, guiding purpose and a sense of identity. Certainly, Cash Craft philosophy values these perquisites highly enough to rank career success as a key milestone on the path to money maturity. Immersed in (or retired from) careers, my investment club mentors not only exemplified professional success, but regarded the career path as the likeliest means by which an aspiring *rentier* could attain both the high income and high savings rates necessary for higher money milestones. However, to their way of thinking, the career milestone ranked as an "apprentice stage" achievement, one trumped by the final goal of financial freedom and early retirement. A simple question often sufficed to determine if careerists really valued the perquisites of the occupational path: *If you knew you only had a year to live, how would you spend your time?*

If the answer to that question involves something other than rendering services for highly taxable earned income, a career might not rank so highly in the asset category after all.

The Metrics of Financial Limitation

For the income investor seeking to build a retirement portfolio, financial abundance provides an aspirational guidepost, denoting a lifestyle much more robust than that of the retiree who merely "gets by." To properly orient our aspirations, let's ponder what it means to "get by." Even for people whose wealth extends solidly into six-figures, a confident retirement often happens late in life and depends upon substantial infusions from social security. The typical monthly retirement income, according to 2017 data, hardly exceeds $2,600. Annualized, this amounts to only $31,200, about double the 2017 Federal Poverty Guidelines for a family of two. In fact, it approximates the income of someone working full-time at sixteen dollars an hour. If any sales associates, customer service reps, or office clerks relish the prospect of a retirement lifestyle based on the income from a $16 per hour full-time job, I invite them to spend a month in a major American metropolis, which will quickly convince them that the average retirement income provides a below average lifestyle. In Southern California, where I live, this amount barely entitles the recipient to survive, let alone thrive. A couple can easily spend 3K per month just on housing and groceries. Home ownership might reduce, but not eliminate, the cost. Property taxes, insurance, upkeep, community association fees and utilities ensure that those without mortgages still face substantial housing-related expenses. Add healthcare, transportation, plus an occasional entertainment or social activity, and the average retirement income quickly loses its luster.

Of course, the world's pattern of relative wealth translates to relative costs, and the budget that means subsistence in Los Angeles, New York, or San Francisco might provide happy existence in Las Cruces, New River, or San Jacinto. Geographic arbitrage provides a time-honored enhancement to the lifestyles of America's retirees, allowing them to stretch pensions and social security payments inadequate for high-cost locales. Promoted in recent years as a "lifestyle hack" by early retirement bloggers, the term hints positively about the joys available to ordinary Americans who relocate to Mexico, or an RV, or perhaps a cabin "off the grid," where bug spray and a spirit of rugged individualism help the retiree tolerate the wilder edges of the world (and perhaps blog about the experience for eager followers). Pursued willingly, in a spirit of adventure, geographic arbitrage provides an expansion to the lifestyle envelope and offers the consolation that a sunset looks just as pretty when viewed from a cabin as from a mansion—provided the mansion doesn't block the cabin dweller's view.

Exhortations conveyed in print lose much of their dramatic effect, particularly if the sentiments so expressed pose a challenge to cherished notions. The investor who quests for leanFIRE, and who finds in these pages a critique of leanFIRE philosophy, will likely raise a shield of counter arguments against Cash Craft ideas of abundance. If, aged thirty to forty, the leanFIRE aficionado already holds the resources—a portfolio, say, of $500,000—necessary to make leanFIRE dreams a reality, then the shield may come burnished with pride. Blessed with good health and the optimism of self-confidence, a person aged thirty-something may well regard $500,000 as "F-U money," a ticket to a life untainted by the constraints of the cubicle.

The wisdom of hindsight gives me a perspective that I hope the F-U money-minded will consider. Viewed from the Realm of Seven Figures, 500K represents not so much a ticket to paradise than a fork in the road. On one hand, it opens the door to sustainable (albeit frugal) adventure away from the rat race. On the other hand, for those who remain in the race, it opens the door to more robust cash flow. Choosing the latter path, I doubled my 500K to a million dollars in just under seven years. Along the way, I stopped thinking in terms of F-U money and more in terms of money momentum, a benefit I could gain by embracing the system rather than dismissing it. In time, the sum I initially regarded as F-U money looked more like false summit, an achievement worthy of note but whose chief value lay in its position as a vista point on the road to higher attainments.

To their credit, many advocates of leanFIRE recognize the opportunity cost inherent in their quest and offer a philosophical perspective to make that cost more palatable. Quitting the cubicle, they contend, doesn't mean an end to work. Rather, it means an opportunity to work on terms agreeable to oneself.

Case History: F-U Money Mistakes

Debbie and Marlon, a thirty-something couple casually associated with the investment club, provide a case history for work-optional living. An attorney with a downtown firm, Marlon voiced frustration with eighty-hour weeks and office politics, a frustration that bred resentment when the firm refused to grant him partner status. At that point, the couple unveiled their F-U money—about $450,000 in mutual funds and real estate equity—which they liquidated to fund their escape. After purchasing a used

RV, Marlon deployed the remainder of their assets into an income portfolio that produced about $2,000 per month—enough, they figured, to fund years of nomadic RV lifestyle. If they needed additional cash, Marlon assumed he could do freelance legal consulting online and Debbie could follow her passion of writing travel articles.

The investment club criticized the plan's opportunity cost, noting how the combination of the couple's net worth and Marlon's six-figure salary needed only a little time to produce powerful synergies. Undeterred, the couple embarked on their plan, and for a while sent club members a glowing correspondence, replete with pictures of famous locales, alluring landscapes, and acquaintances met on the RV trail. Then, the correspondence ceased, leaving the couple's status a mystery.

Some years later, entirely by chance, I encountered Marlon at a gas station in West Los Angeles. Though evasive at first, Marlon confided that he and Debbie had split; unable to fund leanFIRE on his share of the net worth pie, he had returned to "the gripes of the grid." Unfortunately, his time away from the legal grind set him back professionally, and he found himself scrambling to earn half his former income. Since my own portfolio had by that time swelled to nearly a million dollars and produced over $4,000 in monthly cash flow, I remained circumspect about the difference a handful of years made in our finances, lest Marlon see me as an unpleasant reminder of an alternative road.

I have no doubt that for every story like Marlon's, another awaits telling, one whose protagonist successfully converts F-U money into years of leanFIRE inspiration. From a portfolio perspective, I take issue not with the possibility of leanFIRE success, but rather the opportunity cost that work-optional living can't sugar-coat. Though exhortations conveyed in print may lose their dramatic flair, I wonder what exhortations Marlon might invoke, if only he could mail a letter to his younger self. With hindsight, the money that he flashed as a middle-finger gesture to the system proved less meaningful than hoped.

The Metrics of Comfort and Affordability

If we want a budget that allows us to do more than "get by," or that doesn't force us to employ "lifestyle hacks" to conjure financial freedom from the equivalent of an office clerk's salary, we must climb further up the wealth pyramid, into regions occupied by the global top 1%, where the minimum requirement for admission entails wealth ten times greater than the median U.S household. An address in the top 1% means more than a nice view of the wealth pyramid. Financial planners recommend that retirees attain a nest egg equivalent to ten times their final salary. Applying this recommendation to the average U.S. household, whose annual income averages roughly $75,000, we find that a 750K nest egg—*in theory*—represents the gateway to a comfortable retirement. With inputs from social security averaging $1,300 per month, the retiree with $750,000 comes close to absorbing the $56,000 annual cash burn of the typical U.S. household. If he/she has the benefit of a nest egg invested for cash flow, the $56,000 yearly budget comes easily within range: $15,600 from social security, plus $40,400 from investment income, an easily attainable 5.3% yield on a 750K portfolio.

A simple premise underlies the assertion that a budget of $56,000 represents the threshold of a comfortable retirement. This number denotes the annual expenses of a typical American household and, by implication, buys a standard of living most Americans find comfortable. With a $4,660 monthly expenditure, the budget supports a lifestyle three-and-a-half times better than the Federal Poverty Guidelines for a family of two and equates very closely to the monthly take home pay of a worker earning $38 dollars per hour. Put simply, if your income through passive sources buys what most Americans seek through sweat, debt, and a paycheck-to-paycheck existence, you occupy an admirable place in the wealth pyramid.

But, it's still not financial abundance.

Some investors may express surprise upon learning that a person could amass wealth greater than 99% of the world's adults and yet still fall short of financial abundance. In part the surprise stems from consumer culture psychology, which conditions people to regard money not as capital but as a ticket to a shopping spree. The materialist mind pictures a million dollars and dreams of pleasures the sum might purchase. Sadly, the materialist mind often learns too late one of wealth's subtle truths: having the money to purchase an item doesn't necessarily make that thing affordable. To understand why, we must view affordability not by sticker price, but by the concept of "permanent capital equivalence"—the amount of capital required to purchase an item from dividends alone.

The Concept of Permanent Capital Equivalence

Consider the coffee achiever whose typical weekday morning includes a Starbuck's latte, a habit that costs $100 per month to satisfy. Though this amount may not seem burdensome—particularly when viewed piecemeal as a $3 daily expense—the cost changes dramatically when displayed in terms of its permanent capital equivalence. The capital required to sustainably generate $100 per month ($1,200 annually), if invested at the 6% yield typical of my portfolio, comes to about 20K. For most people, the ability to perceive a $100 per month coffee habit in terms of its 20K permanent capital equivalence requires a shift in thinking so extreme as to comprise an uncomfortable disruption of world view.

My investment club colleagues found the concept of permanent capital equivalence so intriguing that they made it a recurring topic of conversation. A club member in possession of a new car, garment, watch, or other accessory often came under immediate scrutiny as debate ensued over the true cost of the purchase. These debates provided an unusual perspective, rarely prevalent among the less money-minded, about the esoteric accounting by which experienced income investors understand the world.

Clifton, one of the founding members of the investment club, elaborated on the concept as follows: "Measured by their permanent capital equivalence, small every-day purchases like sandwiches or gasoline might prove surprisingly expensive, because their limited utility—in the case of a small soda, perhaps lasting only a few gulps—means the full cost occurs 'up front.' A five-dollar sandwich represents the total yearly dividend output of a hundred dollars invested at 5%. By consuming the sandwich, one effectively neutralizes, for that year, one hundred dollars of permanent capital."

Interestingly, Clifton explained, cars, appliances, and other industrial products might entail a high nominal expense, but the durability of the item defrays the full cost over several years, allowing a given amount of capital to provide long-term dividend input. A $25,000 car might require loan payments of $400 per month. Invested at 5% yields, 100K will produce dividends sufficient for the monthly loan payment. "*In proportion to* its permanent capital equivalence, the $25,000 car costs less than the sandwich," Clifton asserted. "The car purchase requires invested capital only four times its price, while the sandwich, a non-durable item with cost fully realized at time of purchase, requires invested capital twenty times its price."

Clifton went on to observe that items of limited utility sometimes count as necessities, and that our culture of money-worship brainwashes consumers with messages that cloud the difference between necessity and the merely nice. "When people incur debt to purchase limited-utility non-durable items, the hidden costs balloon. The human preference for instant gratification, combined with the pressure to consume, ensures that only a small minority of workers find the patience and discipline necessary to make assets the means by which they afford indulgence."

This, as much as anything, explains how in a world of abundant wealth, there remains a scarcity of wealthy.

The Metrics of Financial Abundance

The Pecuniary Paradox suggests a minimum threshold for the attainment of financial abundance. The fact that a small number of people control the majority of the world's wealth implies that the numbers associated with financial abundance comprise a domain of exclusivity. By definition, any numbers associated with the average—in wealth, income, or expenditure—don't qualify. Yet wealth exists on a continuum, and the numbers associated with average provide a basis from which we can extrapolate the minimum necessary for abundance.

The number thus derived will seem laughably low to the penthouse dwellers of the wealth pyramid, yet still represent an amount so far beyond the reach of most people as to represent a fantasy. If $32,000, two-times the Federal Poverty Guidelines, means "getting by," and $56,000, a budget 75% greater (and 3.5 times the poverty guideline) means "comfort," we can reasonably posit that a budget 75% greater still, or 6.1 times the Federal Poverty Guidelines, means financial abundance for a family of two. These proportions suggest an annual budget of roughly $100,000 as a minimum threshold, a number, coincidentally, very close to the $102,000 that a recent Pew Research Center study, cited by CNBC in 2017, lists as the minimum required to qualify a family of two as upper income. *If, from investments alone, an investor sustainably generates income to cover a 100K annual budget, he/she has financial abundance.*

On a similar level of coincidence, and perhaps more interestingly, the number correlates closely to the "happiness threshold" identified by several surveys and sociological studies. The studies show that while making less than 100K, and especially less than 75K, correlates to incrementally lower happiness, making more than 100K does not produce meaningful happiness improvement. Globally, $95,000 denotes the sweet spot for life satisfaction, while the $60,000-$75,000 range encompasses the peak of emotional well- being.[*]

---

[*] Quentin Fotrell, "Psychologists Say They've Found the Exact Amount of Money You Need to Be Happy," *CBS Marketwatch*, March 4, 2018.

Critics who disparage this sum should remember that, due to the different tax treatments of investment income vs. earned income, 100K of dividends roughly equates to the take-home proceeds of a $150,00 salary. I venture that most early retirees, during their working years, would have found a $150,000 salary quite satisfactory.

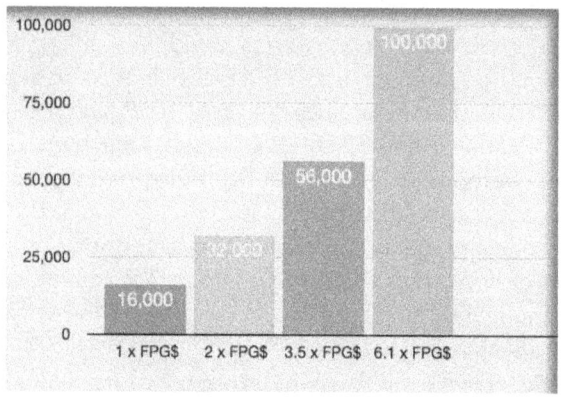

Income levels as a multiple of Federal Poverty Guidelines (FPG) for a family of two

The statistics of global wealth rank this income metric as an exceptional achievement. Very few workers, even those lucky enough to enjoy increasingly rare defined benefit pension plans that provide a promise of substantial salary replacement, can realistically anticipate financial abundance on such terms. The six-figure retirement income, if mentioned in personal finance literature, usually appears as an idealized salary replacement for a target audience advised to work until age seventy in order to maximize social security payouts and IRA distributions. Building such a passive income stream in middle age, without the benefit of inheritance, lottery, or other randomly received capital infusion, merits tremendous acclaim. To reference the wisdom of 17th Century Dutch philosopher Baruch Spinoza, "all things excellent are as difficult as they are rare." So with financial abundance.

Savvy income investors who retain a robust cash reserve and build a portfolio with core assets yielding an average of 6%-7% range will need roughly 1.5 to 2 million dollars to qualify for this minimum threshold of financial abundance. Those willing to embrace a more volatility might supercharge their portfolios with closed-end funds, whose 8%-9%+ yields make the minimum threshold attainable with assets in the 1.4-1.6 million-dollar range. My own portfolio, which tilts toward a more conservative 6% overall yield, achieves financial abundance with roughly two million dollars of assets and net worth equivalence, where "net-worth equivalence" refers to the capital conversion value of a $3,500 per month pension with 2% annual COLA.

Abundance—the Intersection of Philosophy and Finance

Defining financial abundance in specific terms helps untangle the topic from the slick slogans that seem psychologically compelling but offer little in the way of substantive guidance. I recognize, however, that wealth remains a relativistic concept. An attempt to define financial abundance according to specific dollar quantities may invite criticisms of lifestyle bias. In a relative world—assuming one has enough money to provide for basic needs—who can say objectively that happiness exists in some lifestyle circumstances but not others?

An objective inquiry based on references to the wealth pyramid, income levels, and budgets may ultimately matter less to the aspiring retiree than a subjective inquiry about how to best use that most precious of resources—time—which independent wealth, at any level, makes available. Here, where finance intrudes on philosophy, we must acknowledge that even a lifestyle distinguished by its satisfaction of wants has limitations. While the range of human desire extends to infinity, the ability of money to satisfy human desire remains constrained. Some people may want to have a picnic on the moon, and a certain few even possess the resources to do so. However, to indulge the craving on a frequent basis would deplete the wealth of even the wealthiest.

Financial abundance may offer escape from certain aspects of the human condition, but it doesn't help us escape being human. In *Rasselas*, Samuel Johnson tells the story of an Abyssinian prince who left his luxurious valley in search of happiness. "I fly from pleasure," Rasselas tells a sage, "because pleasure has ceased to please." After many adventures he returns, convinced of the futility of finding happiness within the sphere of human experience. While *Rasselas* provides a cautionary tale to those who think riches offer a panacea for Earthly troubles, his example also shows that riches confer a key benefit: time freedom. Ironically, Rasselas' unique position within the range of human circumstance afforded him the rare chance to fully understand the unpleasantry of being human. Financial abundance may not assure the satisfaction of all wants, nor can it assure happiness—yet it does confer that rarest of gifts: complete ownership of one's time.

--Four--

A Meditation on Designing the Income Portfolio

Prelude: A conversation between Mildred and Harold

Mildred: "Look Honey! There go the Smiths, with sunglasses and Panama hats...they must be going on a cruise. Can't we go on a cruise?"

Harold: "Sorry Milly, can't afford it."

Mildred: "Why not? Isn't our portfolio as big as theirs?"

Harold: "Yes...but we hold SCHD, which focuses on quality stocks. They own risky high-yield securities."

Mildred: "Well, they look like they're having more fun than we are."

Harold: "They might have fun now, but over the long run, we'll have a better risk adjusted return."

Mildred: "How do you know that? Five years ago, you promised a new toaster, and I'm still waiting."

Harold: "I can predict the future by looking at the past. Basically, I look at charts and conduct backward-looking simulations."

Mildred: "Backward looking stimulations?"

Harold: "Not stimulations...SIMulations."

Mildred: "I'd rather have STIMulations...like what the Smiths are getting on their cruise."

Harold: "Don't worry Milly. I'll get you a toaster. I'm just waiting for some cap gain, so I can sell an asset."

Mildred: "Sell my a__? What are you talking about!"

※

Early retirees with a penchant for active lifestyles and a cynical regard for the screen-dependent routine of the day trader will find income investing a natural fit to their retirement plans. Prudently designed, the income portfolio requires very little operational monitoring. The stability of income relative to price allows the retiree an aloof detachment from the machinations of the market. I use the word "detachment" intentionally, for it connotes involvement without intensity. Just as the passive collection of rent allows the landlord distance from tenants, so do interest and dividends, swept on a monthly basis from brokerage to bank account, grant the income investor freedom of place and time. Accordingly, the retiree interested in exploring *rentier* life should design a philosophically compatible portfolio.

At its essence, a portfolio—whether designed for income, growth, capital preservation, or some combination thereof—functions as a tool for risk reduction. This basic fact often receives only token attention from mutual fund holders who outsource the details of money management and thus typically care more about results than methods. The idea that a portfolio signifies a *method* deserves some thought. Presumably, an investor blessed with a crystal ball and confidence in its predictions could deploy the entirety of his or her capital into a single investment with great potential and simply wait for the future to materialize. Such foresight would eliminate the need for the insurance policy known as diversification. In a world without reliable crystal balls, fund managers spread their capital among a range of securities that, in sum, implicitly regard the future as a distribution of probable outcomes. Ironically, the occasional sensationalized news stories of people who gain riches by staking everything on a single IPO or penny stock reinforce the wisdom of portfolios. The very sensationalism of such happy endings only highlights their extreme rarity. On a basic level, then, a portfolio represents an attempt to narrow uncertainty into a statistically more probable outcome.

The following list, by no means comprehensive, details some of the risks, arising externally in financial markets and internally in investor psychology, that portfolios attempt to shield:

External Risks

♦*Business Risk*—the possibility that lawsuits, accidents, bad press, or other negative event will disrupt the operations of a company. Witness the Macondo well blowout suffered by BP in 2010 and the wildfire liability suffered by PG&E in 2017-2018.

♦*Industry Risk*—the possibility that technological change, demographic shift, natural disaster, or other existential threat will disrupt an entire industry. Witness the emergence of the Covid-19 pandemic that forced the airline industry to go on government life support in spring 2020.

♦*Management Risk*—the possibility that a visionary CEO might retire, a buffoon gain influence, or a corporate culture fail to recognize change and pursue opportunity. Witness the decline of Kodak, whose management ignored the potential of digital camera technology developed in 1975 by its own engineers.

♦*Market Risk*—the possibility that broad market moves, rather than underlying fundamentals, will determine security prices. Today's trading climate, dominated by "bot-driven" algorithms, confronts the investor with white-knuckle periods of indiscriminate selling (and buying) where prices deviate substantially from normal valuation metrics. Witness the famous "flash crashes" of 2010 and 2015.

♦*Interest Rate Risk*—the possibility that interest rate fluctuations will impact financial markets by affecting the cost of capital, influencing consumer demand, and altering the hedge value of cash-equivalent assets. Witness the "Taper Tantrum" of 2013, when markets roiled with the possibility of rising rates due to changing FED stimulus policy.

♦ *Credit Risk*—put simply, the possibility of default. Witness the 1998 bailout of Long Term Capital Management, whose bond arbitrage strategy imploded in the wake of financial crisis in Asia and Russia, and risked collateral damage to the financial system.

♦ *Sophistication Risk*—the possibility that increasingly complicated financial products dependent on counterparty solvency will derail the financial system. Witness the saga of AIG, whose exposure to credit default swaps during the Great Financial Crisis required it to sell assets in a bid to raise cash.

♦ *Political Risk*—the possibility that legislation or government policy—tariffs, trade wars, and other politically driven acts—will bring uncertainty to financial markets. Witness the municipal bond sell-off in the wake of the 2016 election, when possible tax code changes threatened to make the asset class less attractive.

Internal Risks

As mentioned earlier, some risks arise less from market movements than from individual investor psychology. Often the subject of "behavioral finance," these risks merit an "internal" designation:

♦ *Psychological Risk*—the possibility that fear, greed, impatience, competitive zeal, or other problem of the passions will override objective investment analysis. Doubling down on a losing trade in an egotistical effort to obtain a lower cost basis, striving to hit "home runs" by staking excessive capital on speculative hot stocks, using margin to leverage securities which themselves employ significant leverage—these and other ill-advised acts, to which even experienced investors occasionally succumb, indicate recklessness that a portfolio, with its limits on position size, helps counterbalance.

♦ *Complacency Risk*—the possibility that stable returns and positive economic data will instill a blasé attitude toward impending threats. The relentless rise of U.S. market indices in late 2019 and early 2020, despite hints of a spreading pandemic, highlights investor eagerness to overlook warning signs, especially during a long bull market run. Investors who hedged their equity positions with quality long term bonds suffered much less in the ensuing market crash.

♦ *Perception Risk*—the possibility that lifestyle, social circle, and information source will create a distorted or dangerously biased view of the world. An aristocrat who quips "let them eat cake" upon learning the poor lack bread might suffer from perception risk.

♦ *Decision Risk*—the possibility that a transaction rational under one set of circumstances will carry an adverse financial impact under another. Ian Wilson, the one-time General Electric executive, famously observed that "no amount of sophistication is going to allay the fact that all your knowledge is about the past and all your decisions are about the future." To the extent that past performance data guide investment decisions, we embrace decision risk without a full appreciation of its implications.

To assess the likelihood that these (and other) risks might assail the typical investor, my investment club mentors recommended the "mirror test:" *if you look in the mirror and don't see Warren Buffet. . .*

Prisoners of the present, we plan the future by charting the past. A sense of the wisdom and foolishness of this habit should inform everyone's investment thesis. Income investors seek to minimize foolishness by designing portfolios around an observation—the stability of income relative to price—for which past data provides ample precedent. The manager seeking capital gain can only guess at the amount and source of next year's positive returns. By contrast, the manager focused on income can, under most circumstances, make a very accurate estimate of next year's aggregate dividends and interest. The stability of cash flow lends an element of simplicity to portfolio management. As managers, savvy *incomistas* avoid tampering, and refrain from making a relatively simple operation unnecessarily complex.

The early retiree looking to finance decades of work-optional life may naturally question the merits of self-managing a portfolio. Why not just place capital into a well- regarded fund and let *that* manager worry about the details? Certainly, such products exist. The Franklin Income Fund (ticker: FKINX) boasts a consistent dividend track record dating back to the 1940s. Demographic trends, notably the surge of retiring baby boomers eager to supplement social security with additional passive income sources, create demand for financial products that marketers seek to satisfy. This trend produces an array of mutual funds and ETFs which promise a one-stop-shop of index simplicity combined with enhanced income potential. The Strategy Shares "7 HANDLE Index ETF" (ticker: HNDL) provides a notable recent example. As of this writing (spring 2020), HNDL sports an admirable track record, offering three times the broad market yield* with only one-third the volatility. Whether funds such as HNDL present an adequate solution for early retirees needing to stretch their portfolios over thirty-plus years remains an open question.

My own income investing experience leads me to believe that no single product or fund will suffice for the early retiree who plans to live off portfolio cash long term. Funds that emphasize current yield offer little organic income growth, while funds that promise to "build income" tend to disregard the time value of money. The security that seems compelling under one investment thesis may lose its luster in the context of future alternatives. Add in macro-level concerns—tax code changes, disruptive technologies, etc.—and the prospect of outsourcing wealth management to a single fund, product or adviser lacks long term feasibility. The variety of

---

* Because HNDL links distributions to its NAV, a portion of the "yield" consists of "return of capital" which, so far, has not proved destructive. In the two years between 2018 and 2020, an investment in HNDL has retained its nominal value, despite 24 months of distributions.

income securities, many with unique attributes, combined with the fact that personal needs rarely fit hand-in-glove with fund mandates, make the "one-stop-shop" fund idea a handcuff that limits the exploitation of other compelling cash flow sources.

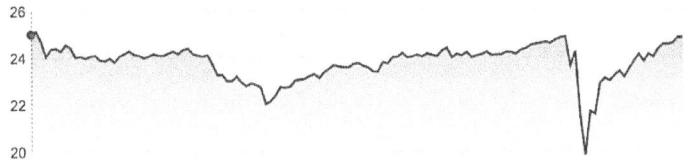

Snapshot of HNDL, showing price action between Jan 2018 and July 2020. Could this very low "beta" fund, dedicated to distributing 7% of its NAV annually, anchor your portfolio? (Chart Data courtesy Google Finance)

In retirement, the income investor confronts two financial imperatives: garnering passive cash flows greater than expenses and growing those cash flows at an inflation-adjusted pace. Equally important, the retiree must adhere to a lifestyle vision that tempers dreams with budgetary practicality. The chief risk likely to confront the well-positioned income investor comes not from external market drama but rather internal psychological and behavioral quirks. Lifestyle inflation—the possibility that a taste for champagne will squeeze a budget built for beer—may well sabotage retirement longevity before monetary inflation ever does.

The prospective *rentier* in possession of sufficient assets will need to consider what yield range, and by implication, what mix of securities, offers the best chance of achieving the aforementioned imperatives. To help inform the decision, Cash Craft philosophy offers three general portfolio designs: "organic growth," "balanced," and "income focused."

Examining the Organic Growth Portfolio

Portfolios designed for organic growth typically yield around 5% and emphasize equities that increase dividends at a pace greater than inflation. Accordingly, the portfolio holds a core of

ETFs and individual stocks which yield more than the market average and sport a lengthy track record of dividend growth. Around this core, the portfolio might include a sprinkling of equity closed-end funds to "juice yield," blended with a dollop of low-yield, low payout-ratio stocks with surging dividends to "juice growth" (i.e. annual income growth). Finally, a fixed-income hedge, plus a cash reserve, amounting to perhaps 10% of total assets, completes the allocation. The following sample portfolio illustrates the type of securities that might fulfill this design:

Allocation	Amount	Ticker	Est. Annual Cash Flow	Annual Income Growth
Core (Specialty ETF)	150K	HNDL	$10,500	$250
Core (Specialty ETF)	150K	SPHD, PEY, QDIV	$7,500	$700
Core (Select Stocks)	100K	O, ABBV, CVX, OKE, MO, Etc.	$5,000	$250
Equity Closed-End Funds	100K	UTG, THQ, BST	$7,000	$150
Select Dividend Growth Stocks	100K	V, DIS, CSCO, MCD, Etc.	$2,000	$200
Bonds	150K	PONAX, BLV, IVOL	$6,000	$0
Bond Closed-end Funds	150K	GBAB, BKT, MGF, PCI, WIW	$10,500	$0
Cash	100K	MINT, LDUR, IVOL, Cash	$1,500	$0
TOTAL	$1MM		$50,000	$1,550

Consciously or subconsciously, income investors who view organic growth portfolios as the solution to the problem of funding a long retirement sympathize with the traditional narrative that equities provide the best defense against inflation. Certainly, historical data paint a compelling portrait of portfolio success fueled by equity returns. Moreover, nothing quite so rewards the dedicated income investor, or uniquely validates the strategy, as a dividend boost. When a company happily owned for its yearly dollar-per-share dividend decides to pay $1.25, a special satisfaction results, especially if the investor considers the amount of fresh capital required to produce the additional income via prevailing interest rates. (A yearly dividend boost of $500 has the same cash flow impact as $10,000 invested at 5%.) Retirees savvy to this math may thus perceive the organic growth portfolio as a regular source of "found money" with substantial value when measured in terms of the base capital otherwise required to generate it.

However, two primary drawbacks dull the shine of organic growth strategies. First, stocks rarely provide dividend growth at *consistently* high rates over the long term. A few years of surging dividend boosts very often give way to several years of plodding growth in the low single digits. The long-term dividend growth rate for equities runs about 5%-6%. Per Rule of 72 metrics, cash flow that increases by average annual rates in the mid-single digits takes between twelve and fourteen years to double. In other words, organic growth portfolios foreground a rosy yield-on-cost expectation that takes years to materialize. This brings up the second drawback: a disregard for the time value of money, the idea that present dollars carry more value than future dollars. To the extent that an emphasis on common stock dividends requires the investor to underweight higher yield alternatives, we might question if dividend growth *on its own* offers a compelling inflation hedge. In the final assessment, bills don't care how they get paid. A fixed income investor able to save a decent portion (say 15%-20%) of annual interest and reinvest the amount in high yielding closed-end funds will also hedge inflation. It bears repeating here that income investors measure success by a simple rubric: whether cash flow covers expenses. Dividend growth provides one tool out of several for accomplishing this.

Examining the Income-Focused Portfolio

On the opposite side of the portfolio design spectrum from "organic growth" lies the "income focused" portfolio. Income-focused portfolios typically yield around 8%-9% and maximize the range of options available in the cash flow investing toolkit. Accordingly, they tilt heavily toward closed end funds, boutique ETFs that concentrate on niche market sectors with above market yields, preferred stocks, and high yielding REITs and MLPs. To the extent that many of these securities have cash flow metrics affected directly or indirectly by interest rates, this type of portfolio represents an assumption about the likely speed and direction of interest rate changes. Closed-end funds, which typically arbitrage the spread between the cost of leverage and yields available in capital markets, often reduce payouts when leverage costs rise substantially. REITs, which retain only a fraction of their operating income, suffer when rising rates increase cost of capital and pressure "cap rates" on new property acquisitions. Preferred stocks, despite their higher yields and priority claim on corporate payouts, lack dividend growth to hedge inflation. As compensation for these risks, the portfolio emphasizes the time value of money, providing up-front cash flow sufficient to grant the recipient a comfortable budget and a surplus for savings/reinvestment. Additionally, tax benefits may accrue from the nature of CEF, REIT, and MLP distributions, a portion of which typically comes to shareholders as a "non-dividend" (and thus non-taxable) payment.

Since this portfolio allocates substantial capital to closed-end funds, a brief overview of the CEF structure may help clarify its potential for income production. Like their more commonly held mutual fund siblings, CEFs hold a basket of underlying securities whose sum price determines fund NAV (net asset value). Unlike mutual funds, CEFs don't redeem shares at NAV, but rather trade at premiums or discounts (sometimes significantly) on market exchanges. Intended to function as pools of permanent capital, CEFs allow managers to pursue fund mandates without regard to the frenzied psychology of investor buying/selling or a need to keep cash on hand to meet redemptions. Additionally, the "permanent capital" aspect of CEFs allows managers to invest more confidently in specialized securities—private placement offerings, private equity, real estate*, etc.—and lever returns while hedging risk through sophisticated tools like swaps and repurchase agreements. (CEFconnect.com, a website specializing in closed end funds, offers excellent historical data on fund distributions and premium/discount averages.) As one might expect, benefits come with drawbacks, and two significant drawbacks confront the CEF investor. First, their leverage and relative illiquidity mean CEFs react with disproportionate volatility to broad market swoons. A decline that reduces stock prices by 30%, as happened in spring 2020, might cut CEF trading prices (as opposed to NAV) by half. Second, because CEFs sometimes pay out more than they earn, and because substantial hits to their NAV may force them to "de-lever" in order to comply with regulatory requirements, a CEF may on occasion suffer a *permanent* reduction in NAV. For these reasons, financial advisors generally recommend that clients limit their CEF allocation to around 15%-20% of a portfolio.

As with most aspects of the investing world, a closer inspection reveals subtleties that well-informed investors can exploit. Not all CEFs behave badly during downturns, and some actually hedge volatility. The Blackrock Income Trust (BKT), for example, remained a bulwark of stability through the Spring 2020 Covid crisis, all the while maintaining its regular monthly distribution. Aware of the nuanced possibilities in the CEF space, my investment club colleagues allocated 50% or more of their portfolios to CEFs, and some relied on CEFs exclusively for their retirement income. The outsized yields (collectively in the 8%-9% range) offered both a budgetary benefit and an intriguing alternative to the withdrawal rate dogma of mainstream finance.

---

* A classic example showcasing the benefits of private placement occurred in the aftermath of the 2008-2009 financial crisis, when investment companies collaborated with the government to launch CEFs built around "PPIP" (public/private partnership) mortgage bonds.

Before rushing to build an "income focused" portfolio yielding 8%-9%, the aspiring *incomista* should remember one of investing's fundamental truths: true risk tolerance often remains unknown until a "black swan" event—a deviation well outside the standard range—exposes fault lines that normal markets leave concealed. By this I do not mean to imply that the income-focused portfolio holds fundamentally greater risk; rather, it presents *unique* risk.

As with most platitudes, the phrase "high yield means high risk" represents an oversimplification that ignores important questions. At what yield threshold does high risk begin? When, after repeated financial crises, devotees of index ideology consider the 4% rule too aggressive and ponder the merits of a 3% drawdown, objective definition of high yield remains problematic. I mention my club colleagues' successful management of income-focused portfolios not to endorse the approach but to verify that some investors do in fact sustainably implement yield-driven strategies not often recommended by mainstream finance. From observation and experience, I recognize the degree of oversight this approach requires and conclude that for most retirees it does not offer a "set it and forget it" comfort. My club colleagues who practiced this approach spent significant time monitoring financial statements, trading trend data, CEF premiums/ discounts, leverage ratios, and other details that might hint at future developments. They engaged in frequent trading and kept substantial cash in reserve. Though dismissive of the premise that high yield means high risk, they embraced the idea that *high yield means high maintenance*.

In practice, the retiree best positioned to tolerate the leverage and likely NAV erosion (not to mention income erosion—a topic I address later) of a portfolio heavily tilted to CEFs is one who has the assurance of future supplemental income stream via pension, social security, or another guaranteed source. Garnering nominal yearly cash flows of 80K-90K from a million dollars of capital doesn't pose a major problem. The challenge arises in hedging that cash flow for inflation, especially in the second decade of retirement, when the annual COLA requires an increase of several thousand dollars. With a decent pension or social security income to supplement portfolio cash flows, this task turns more feasible. Aged 50, the retiree with a million dollars and the prospect of pension/Social Security income at age 62 (the earliest eligible age for Social Security) might deploy capital as follows:

Allocation	Amount	Ticker	Est. Annual Cash Flow	Annual Income Growth
Specialty ETF	150K	HNDL, KBWD	$13,00	$150
Common & Preferred Stock	100K	NLY, MAIN, CHSCO, NLY.D, SFL Etc.	$8,000	$0
Quality Low-volatility CEFs	150K	BKT, MGF, FAX, GBAB, WIW, BHK.	$11,000	$0
Fixed-Income CEFs	150K	PCI, PKO, PTY, PFN, CHI, BIT	$15,000	$0
"Fund-of Funds" CEFs	150K	FOF, RIV, OPP	$17,000	$0
Equity CEFs	150K	UTG, AIO, GOF, JPI, ETY, ETG, PDT, Etc.	$14,000	$50
Cash	150K	MINT, LDUR, GNMA, IVOL, cash	$3,000	$0
TOTAL	**1MM**		**$81,000**	**$200**

Though other allocations and tickers might suffice, no amount of tinkering will remove an inconvenient truth: the portfolio embraces volatility-prone securities to a degree that requires nimble management to preserve capital. In my view, income investing loses much of its benefit when it places the retiree in such an active managerial role.

Balanced Portfolios: The Quality/Productivity "Sweet Spot"

While no retiree significantly exposed to financial markets can truly adopt a "set it and forget it" mentality, a happy medium exists between passive nonchalance and the active oversight required of professional money managers. The retiree interested in sleeping well at night while generating superior yields will find such a medium via the "balanced" portfolio design. According to Cash Craft standards, balanced portfolios typically yield 6%-7% and mix organic growth with (relatively) high current income. In effect, balanced portfolios combine elements of the aforementioned styles to create decent yield with an inflation hedge.

If the balanced portfolio mutes the benefits of the alternative designs, it more significantly mitigates their risks, a feature of compelling interest to the early retiree. In my view, the balanced portfolio represents the quality/productivity "sweet spot," providing the best assurance of robust, low maintenance cash flow for the long term. Partly this opinion stems from the observation, noted by my club colleagues and verified through my own investment career, that despite oscillations in economic activity and interest rates, reliable yields in the 6%-7% range await the investor willing to seek them. Additionally, the opinion derives from a basic total return assumption, i.e., that long term investment results correlate to the sum of GDP + market yield + inflation. Projecting into the future the trajectory of recent historical trends—2% GDP, 2-3% market yield, and 2-3% inflation—we see the 6%-7% yield of the balanced portfolio as essentially a cash flow conversion of economic fundamentals.

Regarding the sum of GDP, market yield, and inflation as a guidepost for charting sustainable cash flows should not raise eyebrows. Managers of pension funds and endowments rely on similar assumptions when modeling future returns. Essentially, it represents an economic translation of the Gordon Growth Model, with broad data used in place of company-specific information. However, the premise that reliable 6%-7% yields exist throughout the economic or interest rate cycle may well challenge conventional wisdom, especially in light of the "ZIRP" (zero interest rate) policy that the FED seems perpetually destined to implement. Critics may question the term "reliable," which, strictly interpreted, refers to income produced by treasury and agency bonds.

Though I fully concur that treasury bonds represent a gold standard for quality and often provide the only safe harbor in times of crisis, they hardly hold a monopoly on the production of steady income. The following CEF data, derived from a 2016 study conducted by my investment club colleagues, hints at the yield possibilities available to investors willing to adopt a more flexible definition. The data reflect averages for the twenty-one years between January 1995 and December 2015, a timeframe, importantly, that encompasses two recessions, a "lost decade" for stocks, and Fed funds oscillations ranging between 6.5% on the eve of the dot-com bust to zero in the wake of the Great Recession.

Ticker	21-Year Avg. Price	21-Year Avg. Income/Share	21-Year Avg. Yield
PDT	$10.65	$0.87	8.1%
AWF	$12.22	$1.33	10.8%
RCS	$10.54	$1.00	9.5%
VKI	$11.82	$0.78	6.6%

A one million-dollar investment in these respective funds generated the following yearly incomes between 1995-2015: PDT, $81,734; AWF, $108,834; RCS, $94,876; VKI, $65,989.

Collectively, the funds held assets ranging from utility preferred stocks to corporate, municipal, and government agency bonds and produced an average of $87,858 per year on a million-dollar investment. Interestingly, an investor with a two-fund concentration of PDT and AWF received an average of $96,237 per year between January 1995 and December 2015, and began 2016 with a portfolio that preserved, at least in nominal terms, the original million dollars.

Though the study focused on long term CEF performance—a matter of obvious relevance to the subset of my club colleagues with heavy CEF allocations—it contained other curiosities, which I present here:

10-Year Returns, 11/29/2005-11/29/2015

Ticker	Annualized Total Return, 2005-2015	Growth of $1,000, 2005-2015
VWINX	7.08%	$1,981
SPY	7.39%	$2,039
CHS 8% Coupon Pfd)	9.01%	$2,369

I take major interest in the fact that, over ten years, an 8% "coupon" preferred stock from Cenex Harvest States (CHSCP) outperformed both the 5-star conservative allocation Wellesley Income Fund and the "efficient market" S&P 500 index fund. The "high yield" preferred stock delivered more return per investment dollar, making it a more ideal intersection of quality/productivity for retirement portfolios than the more "conservative" options.

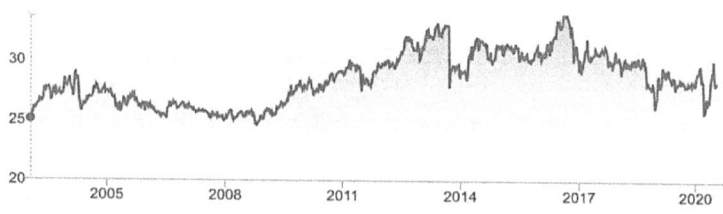

Price performance of CHSCP, the 8% "coupon" preferred stock of Cenex Harvest States. Note the tendency of the security to trade at a premium to its $25 par value, even during the 2008-2009 credit crisis. A 10K investment at par produced $800 dollars per year of dividend income (at tax-advantaged qualified rates) since inception. (Chart data courtesy Google Finance.)

The curiosity grows when we compare the twenty-year performance of VWINX and SPY against the aforementioned specialized CEFs:

20-Year returns (1995-2015)

Ticker	Annualized Total Return, 1995-2015	Growth of $1,000, 1995-2015
VWINX	7.97%	$4,652
SPY	8.37%	$5,012
PDT	9.42%	$6,081
AWF	12.26%	$10,613

Of interest here: the fact that, over twenty years, a pair of levered, relatively illiquid, and volatility-prone CEFs outperformed the SPY index and balanced Wellesley funds, and did so with an emphasis on high-yield debt (AWF) and the preferred stock of utility companies (PDT). (For more information on these funds, consult the supplemental reference at the end of this chapter.)

I present this data as an invitation for readers to consider the possibility that "high yield" and "reliable income" need not comprise mutually exclusive terms. Moreover, I offer the data to suggest that the 6%-7% yield range actually represents a relatively conservative application of income investing potential.

In light of this contention, and sentiments expressed in other meditations, the reader might ask if I regard Cash Craft philosophy as a refutation of the 4% rule and other mainstream retirement advice. Actually, the information and experience gleaned from my affiliation with the investment club makes me question the assumptions behind any investment approach. I don't wish to dispute the 4% rule so much as instill in the reader an open mind to viable alternatives. The better question might proceed as follows: *can a retiree derive an inflation adjusted income 50%-75% higher than what the 4% rule prescribes and still sleep well at night?* I answer "yes," and offer the following sample "balanced" portfolio as one possibility, using allocations and securities modeled on my own portfolio, effective spring 2020:

Allocation	Amount	Ticker	Est. Annual Cash Flow	Annual Income Growth
Specialty ETF	200K	HNDL	$14,000	$350
Equity ETF	200K	SPHD, PEY, QDIV	$10,000	$500
Bonds & Preferred Stock	200K	PONAX, VFIIX, BLV, IVOL, CHSCP, NLY.F, VGLT	$8,000	$0
CEFs (Variety of Equity & Fixed Income)	300K	UTG, BST, THW, ETG, OPP, JRI, RIV, PDT, BKT, BHK, MGF, PCI, PFN, PHK, PTY, GOF, WIW, GBAB, RNP, IGR, ETY, ETW	$27,000	$350
Cash	100K	MINT, LDUR, GNMA, IVOL, cash	$2,000	$0
TOTAL	1MM		$61,000	$1200

Assuming common stock dividends supply 40% of portfolio cash flow, and assuming a conservative 5% dividend growth rate—the low end of the historic trend—the retiree should come very close to achieving the $1,220 budget COLA for retirement year two, given 2% inflation. With half its capital allocated between cash, quality fixed income, and a low-volatility ETF (HNDL), the portfolio amply hedges market downturns while retaining enough equity exposure to generate modest NAV growth. Though vulnerable to NAV hits in the range of 15%-20% during a "black swan" deviation such as transpired in spring 2020, the portfolio offers an income stability that well balances the risk/reward ratio.

Oddball Alternatives: Portfolio Design in Context

In the introduction to this book, I wrote that my investment club colleagues "adhered to, and succeeded with, yield-driven strategies most financial planners consider highly unorthodox." Concerning the aforementioned portfolio styles, I amend this statement with an important caveat: successful implementation of a strategy does not negate the risk involved. Rather, to paraphrase famed Oaktree manager Howard Marks (in turn paraphrasing Nassim Taleb), it merely signifies the investor attained one outcome from a range of possible alternatives.

To say investors "generate returns" ascribes too much agency to their role in the final outcome. Recognizing how randomness underlies probability distributions, we might more accurately regard returns as what happens "when the future collides with a portfolio." Randomness enhances the possibility that asset performance may not correlate to investor expectation. The quest for a magic portfolio capable of optimizing assets while minimizing random outcomes inspires so much financial market scholarship that investors rarely question why a portfolio requires financial market exposure in the first place. Suppose a retiree could obtain a result comparable with the 4% rule yet avoid financial market risk entirely? As an interesting thought experiment, the "Mason-jar Portfolio" almost fits this profile. I mention it for the perspective it lends the current discussion.

Examining the Mason-jar Portfolio

Assuming a 2% inflation rate (the Federal Reserve target rate as of spring 2020), an all-cash portfolio supports a 3% real withdrawal for over twenty-five years. With a million dollars of capital, the retiree could place $30,000 in the Mason jar labelled "Retirement Year One," $30,600 in the jar labelled "Retirement Year Two," $31,212 in the jar for year three, and so on as appropriate for expected COLA (the jar for Year 25 would contain $48,252). For those interested in a bit more excitement, the Mason-jar portfolio would sustain a 4% real withdrawal for over twenty years (again assuming 2% inflation), by which time $971,810 would be spent, leaving the retiree with roughly 28K to splurge on a final party in Year 21.

"Mason Jar Portfolio" Depletion Rates

2% Inflation	3% Inflation
3%+COLA= 25 years	3%+ COLA= 23 years
4%+COLA= 20 years	4%+ COLA= 19 years
5%+COLA= 17 years	5%+ COLA= 16 years
6%+COLA= 14 years	6%+COLA= 13 years
7%+COLA=12 years	7%+COLA= 11 years

Substitute bank CDs for Mason jars, a prudent move that carries the benefit of FDIC insurance, and the numbers turn rosier; a laddered maturity of 2% CDs would sustain a 4% real withdrawal for twenty-five years.

The Mason-jar Portfolio leads to some important observations relevant to portfolio management and design. First, from the standpoint of risk-adjusted return, portfolios designed according to 4%-rule guidelines don't confer a meaningful advantage until much later in retirement, mostly because the inflation risk hedged by financial markets matters more over the long run than over short or intermediate time frames. Second, we can infer that when yields on cash equivalents rise to a point where a "risk-off" trade supports the same withdrawal rate as a "risk-on" trade, the prospect looms of poor risk-adjusted return. Exactly such a situation transpired on the eve of the 2008-2009 financial crisis, when the 5% yields available from bank CDs more than doubled the 2% yield of the S&P 500. (Conversely, the ZIRP rates prevalent since 2009 made financial markets comparatively more appealing.) Third, it hints at how much cash an income portfolio must generate to cover certain spending scenarios without selling shares. The $971,890 that a Mason-jar retiree spends after twenty years (assuming a 40K initial budget) translates, in an income portfolio, to an average of $48,574 annually, roughly a 4.8% yield on a million dollars, to fund both spending and maintain productive potential.

Initial Draw	20-Year Total	Annual Avg.	Avg. Yield
$40,000 (4%)	$971,890	$ 48,514	4.85%
$50,000 (5%)	$1,214,124	$ 60,706	6.1%
$60,000 (6%)	$1,457,822	$ 72,891	7.3%
$70,000 (7%)	$1,713,172	$ 83,658	8.6%

Since the significant effects of inflation take hold in the third decade of retirement, a more prudent estimation relies on the thirty-year projection, during which time the retiree with a 40K initial budget spends $1,621,686, or a yearly average of $54,056 (a 5.4% yield). Running the numbers for higher budgets reveals the somewhat narrow window of withdrawal rate safety applicable to thirty-year time frames. Assuming a fairly benign 2% inflation rate, we derive the following projections:

Initial Draw	30-Year Total	Annual Average	Avg. Yield
$ 50,000 (5%)	$ 2,026,816	$ 67,560	6.75%
$60,000 (6%)	$ 2,524,190	$ 84,139	8.4%
$70,000 (7%)	$ 2863,297	$ 95,443	9.5%

Comparing the budget for Retirement Year One to the budget for Retirement Year Thirty provides another way to look at it. After thirty years with a 2% COLA, the budget of the 4% retiree grows to a $70,000 annual expenditure, while that of the 7% retiree requires over $125,000.

Initial Budget	Budget after 30 Years (2% COLA)
$ 40,000	$ 70,016
$ 50,000	$ 88,700
$ 60,000	$ 106,546
$ 70,000	$ 125,528

In terms of actual dollars produced and the type of assets likely to produce them, growing cash flow in a manner that transforms a 70K annual budget into 125K after thirty years exerts a much different burden on a million-dollar portfolio than transforming 40K into 70K. The 9.5% average yield required to produce the $2,863,297 in total 30- year cash flow for the 7% retiree seems a high hurdle in today's low-yield world. High, *but not impossible*...as the aforementioned CEF study shows, some funds have provided such an average yield, and over a time frame long enough to merit consideration.

Here the broad-market index devotee might raise an obvious criticism: the possibility of an occurrence gives no indication of its likelihood. Though some securities do indeed outperform in a manner supportive of higher withdrawal rates, how many retirees possess the foresight to identify them in advance and allocate sufficient capital accordingly? How could a retiree in 1994 know that a million dollars allocated to closed end funds like PDT and AWF would produce an average of $96,237 per year between January 1995 and December 2015 and retain its nominal value? In truth, the hypothetical retiree couldn't *know* it—but did an investment in such funds really require unusual clairvoyance?

Not too long ago, an assumption prevailed among money managers that, over time, the market ought to provide an annualized total return in the neighborhood of 10%. Capitalizing on this assumption, the Zweig Total Return Fund (ZTR) launched in 1989 with the intent of paying investors 10% of NAV annually*. More recently, personal finance guru Dave Ramsey, citing data from 1923-2016, posits a 12% return expectation for the S&P. Wharton professor and author Jeremy Siegel, citing 200-year data, suggests a more restrained 7% real return—roughly 10% nominal. It bears mention that people who play in the options markets, private equity, and private real estate routinely expect annual returns in the double-digit range. (It also bears mention that devotees of broad market index funds don't *know* the future long-term outcome of their strategy.) In light of these perspectives,

---

* Thirty years later, the fund still exists, though shareholders have found that 10% distributions don't always mean 10% total returns.

attaining withdrawal rates higher than those deemed possible by broad market indexers hardly requires fortunate security selection. Rather than ascribe clairvoyance to retirees whose portfolios outperform, we might pose a more relevant question: how much of a higher withdrawal rate can a retiree sustain by concentrating capital in specific market sectors rather than broad indexes?

If we define risk as the potential gap between investor expectation and likely asset performance and admit that higher withdrawal rates exert progressively higher demands on inflation-adjusted cash flow, then risk grows considerably, especially in the third decade of retirement, for rates higher than 7%. An 8% withdrawal rate, sustained for thirty years, implies yield averages into double digits. To the extent that long term total returns reflect the sum of GDP + broad market yield + inflation, an expectation for such double-digit averages seems overly optimistic, at least in light of current data.

From the discussion so far, the reader may infer why I consider the 6%-7% yield of the "balanced" portfolio an ideal intersection of quality and productivity. Below 5%, the tilt toward higher quality doesn't make up for the opportunity cost of ignoring reliable up-front cash. Below 4%, the merits of exposing assets to financial market risk come into question entirely. On the other hand, an expectation of 8% or higher challenges the retiree with the prospect of nimble portfolio management and the likely disparity between nominal cash flows and real cost of living adjustments.

Or does it?

Exploring the 100% CEF Portfolio

In deference to my investment club mentors, who routinely played in the high-yield arena, I here revisit the income-focused portfolio to consider the possibilities that a 100% CEF allocation might offer a fifty-year-old retiree with nerves of steel, a million dollars of capital, and the assurance of pension or social security income by age sixty-two (the youngest eligible-age for social security). Taking a page from the ZTR playbook, and noting that nominal yields in the 10% range always exist somewhere in the CEF space, we might concentrate on a "fund of funds" approach, built around a core of appropriate tickers (RIV, OPP, FOF), supplemented with a selection of others from well-regarded managers (PIMCO, Blackrock, Guggenheim) thrown in for spice, toward a collective 10% yield.

This portfolio, unburdened by a cash reserve or low-yielding treasury bonds to hedge volatility, should produce 100K annually from a million dollars of capital—at least in a theoretical world, where it would support an 8% inflation-adjusted withdrawal for over thirty years (assuming the retiree reinvests the entirety of surplus income--20K--at the 10% nominal portfolio yield). In practice, however, the portfolio will suffer some degree of income erosion over time. Some funds will experience defaults, others will engage in a destructive return of capital that reduces long term income potential, and still others will de-lever during bouts of market turmoil, reducing payouts.

A lack of comprehensive data on the long-term aggregate CEF income erosion presents a complication. Using FOF (the Cohen and Steers Closed-End Opportunity Fund) as a proxy for the space, and noting its pattern of distributions between 2006 and 2020, I *guesstimate* an aggregate CEF income erosion rate of roughly 1.5% annually. To counter this, the retiree could redeploy all income not needed for expenses back into the portfolio, to produce income for the following year at the nominal 10% rate. Assuming 2% inflation, an 8% withdrawal, and a million-dollar capital investment, we find the following numbers for retirement year one:

Nominal Income	Withdrawal	Excess	Next Year Addition (Est.)
$ 100,000	$80,000	$ 20,000	$ 2,000

Due to the 1.5% erosion rate, the year 2 nominal income, absent reinvestment, reduces to $98,500. Happily, the reinvested excess offsets the reduction, supplying $2,000 of additional CEF

(10% nominal yield) income, leading to the following Year 2 numbers:

Nominal Income	Withdrawal	Excess	Next Year Addition (Est.)
$ 100,500	$ 81,600	$ 18,900	$ 1,890

and then for Year 3:

Nominal Income	Withdrawal	Excess	Next Year Addition (Est.)
$ 100,882	$ 83,232	$ 17,650	$ 1,765

From these numbers we can deduce the emergent trend. Though able temporarily to maintain nominal income in the 100K range (it goes to $101,240 in Year 5), we can't do so in a manner that keeps pace with needed withdrawals. Each year, the excess income, and consequently the reinvestment hedge, diminishes, until it practically vanishes in Year 11:

Nominal Income	Withdrawal	Excess	Next Year Addition (Est.)
$ 97,882	$ 97,519	$ 363	$ 36

Clearly, the $36 of additional income anticipated for Year 12 will fall short of the $1,950 needed for the 2% inflation-adjusted withdrawal. Lacking an additional cash flow source, the portfolio will experience a death spiral, in which spending rapidly outpaces income and depletes the asset base.

Enter the pension. If, by retirement year 12, the retiree receives an annual pension—say $35,000 with a 2% COLA—and deploys the entirety at the 10% nominal yield of the CEF asset base, the portfolio gains an infusion sufficient to keep the death spiral at bay, as the numbers for years 12, 13, and 14, respectively, indicate:

Nominal Income	Need	Extra	Pension	Amount Reinvest	Next Year's Addition
$96,450	$99,469	(3,019)	$35,000	$31,981	$ 3,198
$101,175	$101,458	(283)	$35,700	$35,411	$ 3,540
$103,506	$103,487	19	$36,414	$36,433	$ 3,643

By Year 14, bolstered by pension cash, the CEF portfolio once again supplies an income in excess of budgetary needs, until by Year 30 it produces over $142,400 to cover a budget of $142,060.

Apart from a miraculous ability to avoid taxes (for simplicity, I left them out of the calculation), the retiree who adopts this approach stakes a tremendous amount on assumptions that deserve greater examination. First, the idea that inflation will average 2% for thirty years might provoke debate, especially in light of recent central bank policies. To this controversy I add only a simple observation: through the course of my investing career, a timeframe dating back to the early 1990s, strident political and economic voices have sounded dire warnings about inflation troubles—and, in doing so, resembled the proverbial boy who cried wolf. (Since 2008, *de*flation has likely posed the greater threat.) Insofar as CalPERS, one of the largest pension funds in the nation, uses 2% as the basis for their COLA assumption, I see no reason to dismiss 2% as misguided. Second, the idea of applying a 1.5% erosion rate to aggregate CEF distributions may seem too off-the-cuff. Though I suspect some investment firms may collect data on the subject, I have no awareness of any publicly available study, and must therefore hazard an estimation, recognizing that some funds boast admirable distribution histories while others make a habit of payout reduction. Using "fund of funds" products like FOF as proxies for the CEF space poses complications, since these funds often engage in trading practices that obscure income-based returns. The variety of CEF inception dates adds another complicating factor, skewing distribution data that might otherwise look worse if limited to long-dated funds. Frankly, anything more than an educated guess might prove elusive. Perhaps the retiree interested in this approach does best to cautiously anticipate *some degree* of aggregate income erosion, recognizing that funds which specialize in certain strategies will incur erosion at more pronounced rates (covered call funds being particularly notorious).

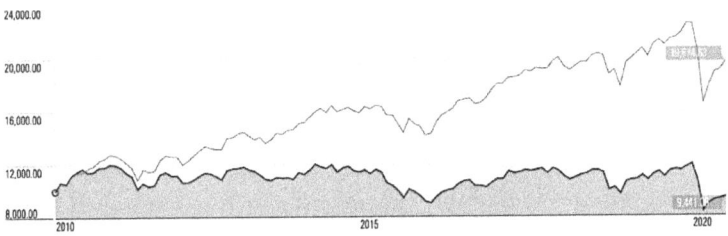

FOF 10K Growth, 2010-2020 (Source: CEF Connect). The top line represents the value of an investment with dividends reinvested, while the bottom grey "mountain" chart indicates share price.

Most retirees will no doubt relegate the 100% CEF portfolio to the same category of amusement as the Mason-jar Portfolio: an interesting mental exercise that in practice entails an approach so unorthodox as to ensure it remains a curiosity. The volatility alone, potentially subjecting NAV to sudden swings of 50% during major market turmoil, makes it incompatible for those who like a good night's sleep. Picture, however, a future of benign inflation and interest rates ideal for levered strategies. Wouldn't such a future warrant a substantial commitment to CEFs?

If we adopt Howard Marks' view and perceive investment returns as what happens when the future collides with a portfolio, then it makes sense to develop a thesis about the distribution of future probabilities. What direction, and at what velocity, will inflation and interest rates change? A glimpse at the Fed Funds Rate chart (courtesy: St. Louis Fed) over the past thirty years shows a significant trend:

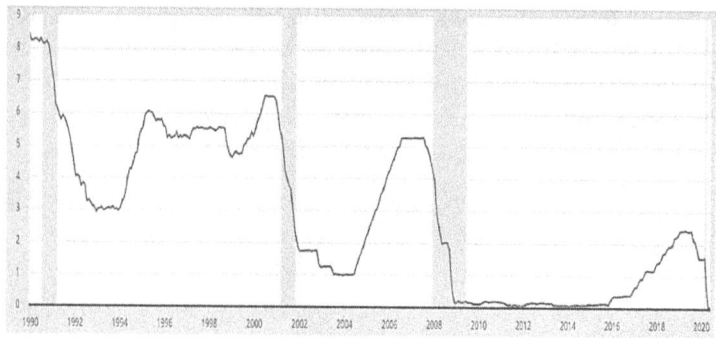

Charting pre-recession highs and stimulus lows suggests that pressure remains inexorably downward. In July 1990, Fed funds rates stood at 8%, and then bottomed at 3% after the 1990-1991 recession. In May 2000, just prior to the "dot-com" bust, rates peaked at 6.5% before descending to the 1% range. In June 2006, just prior to the Great Financial Crisis, rates reached a plateau of 5.25% before declining to ZIRP for nearly a decade. Recently, in December 2018, the Fed managed a relatively puny hiking sequence to 2.5%, only to adopt ZIRP once again in the wake of the 2020 pandemic.

The series of lower highs and lower lows corresponds to the "Great Bond Bull" which prognosticators repeatedly (and prematurely) declare "dead" and from which income investors with rate-sensitive portfolios derive substantial tailwinds. It also reveals a U.S. economy unable to support meaningfully higher rates and increasingly dependent on lower rates. In light of this trend, retirees face a prospect for which history provides little guidance: how to position a portfolio for zero and even negative interest rates. Though markets have a way of rendering prognostications premature, I contend the rate environment offers two obvious implications for managers of income portfolios. First, any sustained sell-off in quality fixed income presents a major buying opportunity, especially for long-duration bonds. Second, the income potential of closed end funds, run by managers adept at maximizing rate arbitrage, suggests that CEFs merit relatively higher allocations in any retiree's portfolio, regardless of design emphasis.

Meditation Four Supplemental References

Exhibit A: "Trinity Study" Withdrawal Rates and Probability of Portfolio Survival

Using Ibbotson's Stocks, Bonds, Bills, and Inflation Data, 1926–2017, S&P 500 and Intermediate-Term Government Bonds

	3%	4%	5%	6%	7%	8%	9%	10%
100% Stocks								
15 Years	100	100	100	90	79	69	67	54
20 Years	100	100	92	82	71	62	48	40
25 Years	100	99	82	72	63	54	40	28
30 Years	100	94	78	67	56	43	37	21
35 Years	100	91	76	59	52	36	26	14
40 Years	100	89	70	55	38	28	21	9
75% Stocks								
15 Years	100	100	100	97	82	72	60	47
20 Years	100	100	95	81	68	53	45	26
25 Years	100	100	84	69	59	47	28	12
30 Years	100	98	78	59	48	37	13	3
35 Years	100	93	69	55	38	26	5	2
40 Years	100	92	66	45	30	6	2	0

50% Stocks

15 Years	100	100	100	100	85	72	50	36
20 Years	100	100	99	79	62	41	27	5
25 Years	100	100	85	60	44	22	7	1
30 Years	100	100	70	46	25	10	2	0
35 Years	100	97	59	34	9	5	2	0
40 Years	100	87	45	17	0	0	0	0

25% Stocks

15 Years	100	100	100	99	77	60	38	19
20 Years	100	100	95	64	47	22	8	1
25 Years	100	100	66	46	22	9	1	0
30 Years	100	87	44	21	10	3	0	0
35 Years	100	71	22	9	7	2	0	0
40 Years	98	45	9	0	0	0	0	0

0% Stocks

15 Years	100	100	99	90	64	38	23	13
20 Years	100	95	77	41	26	11	3	0
25 Years	97	79	38	25	9	3	0	0
30 Years	83	44	22	10	3	0	0	0
35 Years	72	28	9	7	2	0	0	0
40 Years	62	11	0	0	0	0	0	0

Exhibit A Commentary

The numbers offer a few "takeaways," some obvious and others less so:

◆ a 50% stock/bond portfolio stood a 100% chance of funding a 4% real withdrawal rate for thirty years. Put another way, for any rolling thirty-year period within the parameter of the study, following the 4% rule ensured portfolio survival, assuming a 50-50 broad-market stock/bond allocation.

◆breaking the 4% rule did not necessarily break the bank. For example, a 75% stock portfolio stood a 78% chance of funding a 5% real withdrawal for thirty years. A retiree who dared to implement a 5% SWR succeeded in almost four out of every five rolling thirty-year periods.

◆the factors that influence probability of success (in particular, inflation) exert much more influence in the third retirement decade than during the first two. For example, a 6% withdrawal had a 100% chance of lasting fifteen years and a 79% chance of lasting twenty years. Therefore, retirees who have the benefit of non-portfolio cash flow sources (e.g. pension, inheritance, etc.) may well question to what extent the 4% rule applies to them

◆the 4% rule rests on a foundation of several key assumptions: an allocation to broad-market stock & bond indexes, certainty of surviving any rolling thirty-year period, and selling shares to fund cash withdrawals. The numbers do not provide information about the success probabilities of portfolios that concentrate within specific market sectors and which provide sufficient income, from dividends alone, to fund living expenses.

Exhibit B—Select Data for Referenced Closed-End Funds

Growth of 10K, 1998-2020. The top line, depicting 10K growth, reveals the income component (i.e. dividend reinvestment) in CEF total returns, while the bottom line "mountain chart" depicts price behavior alone. (Chart data courtesy CEF Connect.)

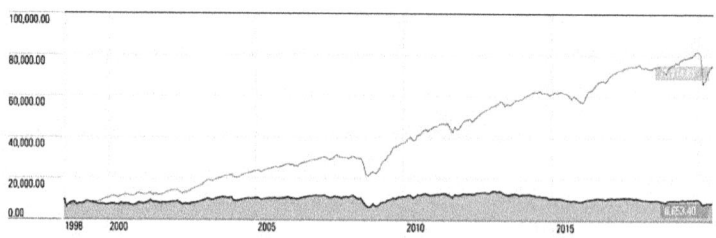

Alliance Bernstein World Dollar Fund (AWF): 10K in 1998 = 75K in 2020.

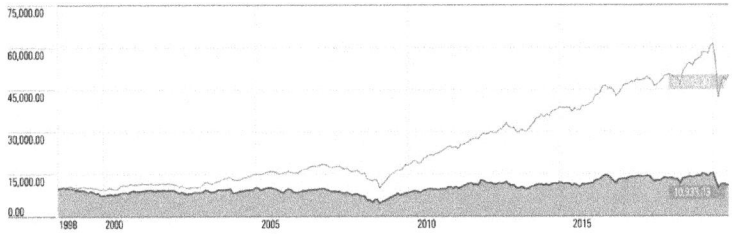

John Hancock Premier Dividend Fund (PDT): 10K in 1998 = 50K in 2020

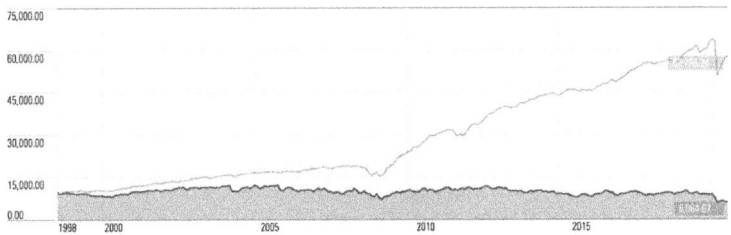

PIMCO Strategic Government Fund (RCS): 10K in 1998 = 57K in 2020

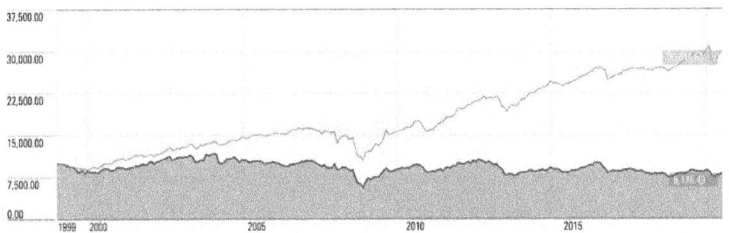

Invesco Municipal Advantage Income Trust II (VKI): 10K in 1998 = 30K in 2020

Exhibit B Commentary

Designed for income production, CEFs will naturally produce total returns derived primarily from the income portion of the TR equation. The five-fold return produced collectively by the referenced funds—a result achieved despite market price declines for AWF, RCS, and VKI—highlights the income potential of the CEF approach. Note that while the income component drives CEF returns, capital gains do play a role, significantly so in some years, when fund managers pass them on to shareholders via "special distributions" equating to several months' worth of regular income, as the following charts, portraying "specials" as spikes in the distribution pattern, indicate (chart data courtesy CEF connect):

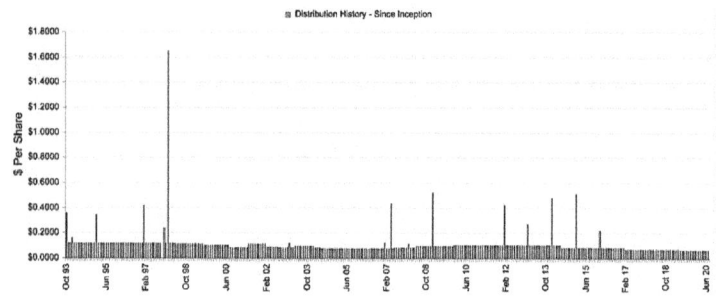

AWF

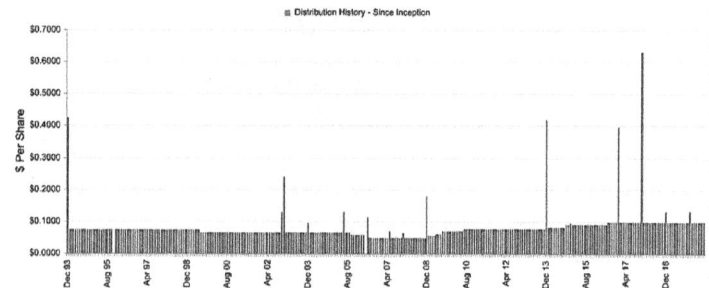

PDT

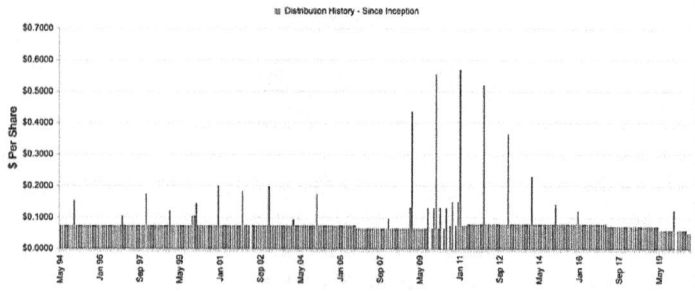

RCS

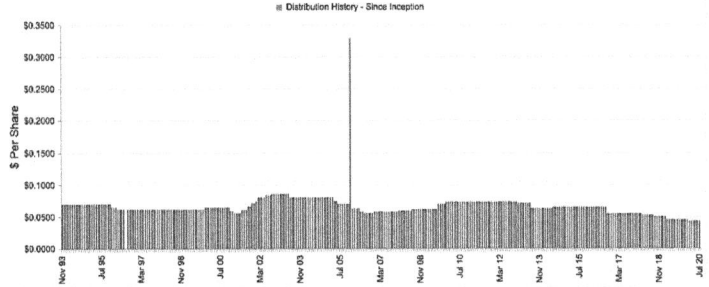

VKI

The multi-decade returns data, plus the diverse security types collectively represented, made the investment club consider the referenced funds good candidates for study. By no means did they consider the funds a representative sample of the CEF space or CEF performance (indeed, some wanted to average the RCS data with other PIMCO funds, such as PTY, PCI, and PDI, to better represent the post-Financial Crisis leverage tools employed by skilled managers.) Nevertheless, the study did convince club members to invest more aggressively in fixed-income CEFs. Ruben, who already ran a 100% CEF portfolio consisting mostly of fixed-income CEFs, regarded the returns data as a critique of investor's fascination with equities. "Fixed income investors didn't suffer a 'Lost Decade,'" he liked to remark, a comment to which he occasionally added a smug footnote: "a retiree with sufficient capital really has no need to slum around in the basement of the capital structure."

When cubicle life you cannot endure
F-U money holds a special allure
Pawn your possessions, recycle your floss
Then raise a middle finger to your boss!
Buy an RV, hype the plan to your wife
Blog about the work-optional life
Sure, the cynics might look down their noses
But they are not out smelling the roses
When the roses wilt in the winter rains
You can blog about how your wife complains!

--Five--

A Meditation on Achieving the Million-Dollar Portfolio

The following meditation, written in late 2017, references data from the 2017 Global Wealth Report, released in the spring of that year by Credit Suisse. (The destructive effect of the 2020 pandemic crisis on global wealth remains unknown at the time this book went to press). Critics of the data contend that Credit Suisse includes illiquid assets such as personal real estate in net worth tallies and thus provides an inaccurate portrait of productive cash-flowing wealth. Investors in possession of million-dollar portfolios thus comprise an exclusive subset of the Credit Suisse data.

In 2017, at the age of forty-seven, I joined ranks with the 36 million millionaires that, according to the Credit Suisse Global Wealth Report for 2017, "comprise less than 1% of the adult population, but own 46% of household wealth." A glance at my resume reveals few attributes of a millionaire-on-the-make. I claim neither a rich uncle nor an ivy-league pedigree. Instead of majoring in a high-demand STEM field, I followed my heart into the Humanities. The eighty-hour weeks, side hustles, and tech-stock tips of the cubicle crowd never appealed to me. Importantly, I never read any of the "millionaire manuals" promoted on personal finance websites. Rather, guided by thrift, patience, and careful investing, my journey to the realm of seven-figures followed a route known since ancient times for its slow yet reliable outcome. As I write this, with plans to pursue early retirement on a passive income of 100K, I think back to the trials and tribulations of my first minimum-wage job, and marvel at the way willpower, adherence to an investing philosophy, and a smattering of luck wrought an impressive result from a humble beginning.

The annals of comparative statistics contain few numbers more interesting to the voyeur than those which reveal our finances. By discussing the details of my own wealth, I perhaps invite the slings and arrows of the comparison curmudgeons, who cynically observe that a million dollars doesn't mean much in a country that abandoned the gold standard for inflationary economics, and who remark that retirement in middle age seems geriatric when computer programmers pursue "early retirement extreme" in their twenties.

The cynics have a point. In an era of devalued dollars and Facebook friends, the foundations of fame sink so low that almost anyone can stake a claim. Moreover, people need nothing near a million dollars to rank highly on the global wealth pyramid. As of 2017, according to Credit Suisse, a net worth of $2,200 grants membership to the top half of global wealth. Ponder that for a moment and consider the implications—debt-free people in possession of a functional automobile, a one-carat diamond ring, or a quality diving watch have more wealth than half the planet's adult population. Those who lack these things but have a job at McDonald's or Walmart (or another establishment paying ten dollars per hour) require just over two months' full-time wages to rank in the top half of the wealth pyramid, provided they save the money.

Two phrases from the above paragraph resonate like subtle alarm bells: *debt-free people* and *save the money*. Interestingly, despite the low bar for membership in the top half of global wealth, the twin shackles of high debt and low savings prove so heavy that many households can't muster the $2,200 entrance fee, but instead have a negative net worth. According to a 2016 Bloomberg study, this predicament describes roughly 15% of U.S. households.

Considering a million dollars in the context of global wealth provides an important way of appreciating its significance. The present political climate creates a polarized distinction between the "one-percenters" who inhabit the top of the wealth pyramid and the 99% stuck in its lower levels. The distinction, and the angst it inspires, glosses over important details about financial habits and perceptions of wealth, notably the fact that those who rise quickly through the wealth pyramid tend to deploy their money into liquid assets that produce cash flow.

Cash Craft philosophy, and the brand of income investing it inspires, focuses on a driving purpose: early retirement on a passive annual income of 100K. Only by amassing substantial income-producing assets can the aspiring *rentier* achieve this goal. Accordingly, the title of this meditation deserves an explanatory addendum. Though the phrase "million-dollar" perhaps entices the reader, the word *portfolio* deserves the most attention, for it highlights the productive potential of the underlying wealth. Put another way, at age forty-seven I didn't just gain millionaire status. Rather, I attained the more important distinction of having a million dollars' worth of income producing assets.

Though an investor might conceivably retire with less, only by possessing income-producing assets of a million dollars or more can he or she hope to sustainably generate cash flow on a par with the after-tax proceeds of a top 10% salary. As such it represents a key net worth milestone, a vista point from which an investor discerns the doorway to meaningful financial abundance.

During my association with the investment club, I often heard the following bit of financial philosophy: *wealth merely represents cash flow subjected to the catalyst of time and good money habits.* As a self-made millionaire, I can attest to the truth of this assertion. Achieving the million-dollar portfolio does not require remarkable talent or rare genius. The traits associated with donkeys—perseverance and determination—will suffice for aspiring millionaires. Moreover, as a resident not of the penthouse but rather the wealth pyramid's less-exclusive top floor, I retain a humble perspective as I ponder my financial journey. Nevertheless, the statistics of global wealth speak for themselves. Workers around the world strive for riches, displaying perseverance and determination, yet find the top levels of the wealth pyramid out of reach. What financial perceptions distinguish the millionaires from those who inhabit the lower levels? An investigation of some key wealth brackets may yield some insight.

Exploring the Wealth Pyramid

Three particular wealth zones—the Five-Figure "Swamp," the low Six-Figure "Hurdle," and the mid Six-Figure "Launchpad"— have crucial importance for the aspiring income investor. The speed at which an investor progresses through them has major implications for the achievement of a *rentier* lifestyle in a realistic timeframe.

For practical purposes, and for the sake of expediency, we can save for another discussion the struggles that take place in the lower levels of the wealth pyramid. The vast majority of the world's adults—and a sizeable percentage of the U.S. population—worry more about economic survival than financial freedom[*]. Cash Craft philosophy presumes that interested students at least have the basic requisites—desire, savings, and a decent (though not necessarily substantial) portfolio—to enable meaningful income investing success. Accordingly, we begin our exploration of the wealth pyramid two levels below the top, a region where people able to reduce debt, increase savings, and insulate themselves from extreme financial challenge fit the profile of the Average American Household.

With a net worth of $76,4165 (2017 data), the aspiring affluent gain a view loftier than the one accessible to 90% of the world's adults. Coincidentally, this price tag correlates to what the Census Bureau lists as the average U.S. household pre-tax income of $73,300. It also correlates closely to the median U.S. household net

---

[*] Ashvin Chhandra's *The Aspirational Investor* (HarperCollins, 2015) references 2013 data to note that "one third of American Families are either already bankrupt or just one cataclysmic event away from complete financial ruin." Despite political propaganda to the contrary, subsequent years have not substantially improved this situation.

worth of $75,000 (the number varies between $70,000 and $80,000 depending on source). These numbers help establish America as one of the richest countries on Earth, and people who find in them a reflection of their personal finances deserve a pat on the back—they have more economic power than nine-tenths of the world's adults. While reflecting on this metric of good fortune, consider that most adults in India and Africa amass less than ten thousand dollars in their entire lives.

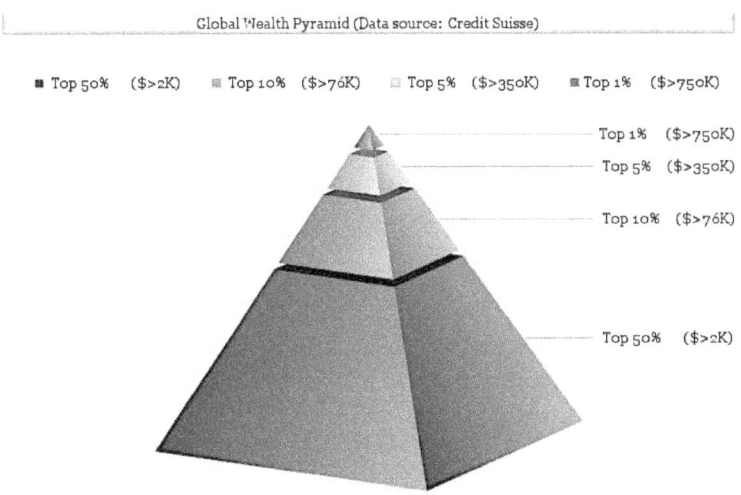

The top half of the wealth pyramid, circa 2017. Data from Credit Suisse reveal the fluctuating nature of these numbers. As of 2019, $7,087 grants access to the to 50%, while $109,430 buys admission to the top 10%

A closer examination of the financial traits associated with this level of wealth reveals a less cause for cheer. With annual expenses over $56,000, according to the Bureau of Labor Statistics, the average American household spends cash nearly as fast as it comes in. Such families muddle from paycheck to paycheck, counting on good fortune to preserve the jobs and health on which their place the wealth pyramid depends. Moreover, with the bulk of their net worth in illiquid "assets" like houses and cars, suffering a job loss or a prolonged illness can initiate a slippery slope of wealth destruction. Recent surveys indicate that nearly half of Americans face difficulty finding a spare $500 for an emergency*. While America ranks among the world's richest countries, most Americans—even those whose net worth surpasses most of the world's adults—don't feel very rich.

Case History: Life in The Five-Figure Swamp

Applying the term "swamp" to five-figure life seems callous but aptly portrays a financial condition where gains more likely accrue from painstaking efforts to save than from market dynamics. Suzie, a self-confessed "Bling Barbie" who sought the advice of my investment club colleagues, fits the profile of life in the Five-Figure Swamp. The equity in her condo comprised the bulk of her $80,000 net worth. After taxes and deductions, the $75,000 gross pay from her job dwindled to $55,000, an amount quickly dissipated by spending and bills, two of which—a lease payment on a BMW and a credit card with a sizeable balance—proved particularly onerous.

Suzie's penchant for showy transportation, clothing, and socializing meant most of her cash flow went to satisfy liabilities rather than build assets. Rationally, Suzie recognized that her consumption choices only deepened the mud which kept her mired in the Five-figure Swamp, yet she confessed that the consumption held a psychological allure, projecting a "feeling" of a lifestyle to

---

* Aimee Picchi, "Most Americans Can't Handle a $500 Surprise Bill," *CBS News*, Jan. 6, 2016. Economists and sociologists tend to regard this situation sympathetically, blaming the cash-deprived state of Americans' bank accounts on decades of wage stagnation. Whether psychological or economic in nature, it offers a reminder of why the *rentier* life proves so elusive. A robust emergency fund represents a basic ingredient for life success, let alone investment success.

which her friends and co-workers considered themselves entitled. This psychology, combined with the emotional reassurance of property ownership, numbed Suzy to the sacrifices required of her if she wished to meaningfully improve her finances.

Like many Americans, Suzy held an unquestioned belief in the merits of personal (as opposed to investment) real estate—an illiquid entity producing no cash flow—and thought that her condo's market appreciation would offset her spendthrift habits. Unfortunately, because Suzie's equity amounted to less than half her condo's assessed value, a ten percent gain in the real estate market could only improve her net worth by four percent, or a bit less than $4,000. By contrast, a savings program, even at the traditionally recommended ten percent rate, could net Suzie over $5,000 from her $55,000 net salary. Typical of people in the Five-Figure Swamp, Suzie lived a paycheck to paycheck existence, and found even a ten percent savings rate too high a sacrifice[*].

Scholars of behavioral finance might highlight the emotional component in Suzie's consumerism, correlating the pleasure she found in spending to her social insecurities. To the investment club, she typified someone whose inability to master "apprentice stage" financial lessons perpetuated a subservient relationship with money. Her attachment to the present clouded a visionary appreciation for the future and the psychological, emotional, and financial steps necessary to create it. Successful wealth builders intuitively understand the emotional component in the act of saving. Positive emotions, and their inspirational power, gain reinforcement when the wealth-builder associates present sacrifice with future well-being.

---

[*] In this, Suzie reflected the perception of money and "success" critiqued by scholars Thomas Stanley and William Danko in their famous 1996 wealth study *The Millionaire Next Door*: "Why are so few people in America affluent? Even most households with six-figure annual incomes are not affluent. . .They believe in spending tomorrow's cash today. They are debt prone and are on earn-and-consume treadmills."

Financial Services Industry Profile of a "Low Net Worth" Household	
Investable (liquid) Assets	Less than $100,000
Income	$50,000
Cash Holdings	$6,800
Leverage Ratio (Debt to Assets)	350%
Likelihood of Direct Stock Ownership	6%
Age	Majority under 55
Households in Cohort	87.3 million
Main Financial Advisory Needs	Debt management, emergency savings

Key financial metrics of a household with less than 100K in liquid investable assets (source: John Hancock insurance/LIMRA). Data reflect averages, effective 2016, for households in the cohort.

Admittedly, showcasing Suzy as the poster child of swamp suffering oversimplifies the variety of issues that beguile people at this level of the wealth pyramid. Life circumstances and negative events may well sabotage aspiring wealth builders who otherwise display six-figure potential. Nowhere in these pages do I imply that financial struggles amount to financial "failures" or that net worth provides a barometer of self-worth. Anyone who has traded hours for dollars on the wage slave treadmill—as I have—knows the indignation that capitalism inflicts on those who lack capital, and retains, subliminally if not explicitly, a sense of empathy for those who remain treadmill-bound. Unfortunately, in the psychology of American consumer culture, money and status equate so powerfully that people feel judged no matter how delicate the terms of financial discussions. The unvarnished truth is that investing requires capital, and a viable income portfolio requires a dauntingly substantial amount. The retiree able to live off dividends and interest will likely always present an economic, social, and political curiosity. As an income investor, I leave the moral implications of rentier life for others to discuss and focus instead on its logistics.

Viewed strictly from an income investing perspective, Suzy's case represents of traits to avoid. Her anemic savings rate, the embrace of credit as a spending crutch, and the willingness to hold the bulk of her wealth in unproductive real estate typify the psychological and behavioral tendencies that prevent progress toward the higher levels of the wealth pyramid. Though escape from the Five-Figure Swamp requires several traits contrary to Suzy, people who quickly achieve escape velocity exhibit two in particular:

♦ *they maintain a robust cash reserve*

The standard financial planning recommendation of an emergency fund equivalent to six-to-twelve months' expenses applies here. Frankly, the recommendation reflects basic prudence more than a wealth building roadmap. At a bare minimum, regardless of financial planning advice, savers should keep $10,000 in a money market or savings account dedicated specifically for emergency need. The ability to maintain a minimum of 10K in an emergency fund provides a telling barometer both of future wealth potential and the likelihood of escaping the Five Figure Swamp in a speedy timeframe. Other cash reserve components, beyond a checking account for recurring expenses, include money held in "cash equivalent" products like bank CDs, money market mutual funds, and high-quality bond funds with short durations. At a minimum, such funds ought to match, and ideally double, the emergency fund. Beyond providing insulation from the vicissitudes of life, a cash reserve encourages the saver to recognize cash *as an asset*, something to acquire and deploy for productive use rather than deplete through spending.

♦ *they strive to place themselves on more equal terms with money*

This second trait describes an underlying mental perspective that helps reinforce the first trait. People who make speedy progress through the Five Figure Swamp develop an early recognition that in the money game they suffer an initial disadvantage: money controls them and grants the pleasure of its company only in exchange for a costly sacrifice of labor and time. Ideally, the desire to rectify this condition inspires a wealth perspective that leads to more solid financial footing. Specifically, the perspective regards savings as a transformation of labor into capital, the seed for future investment-based (rather than labor based) income streams, and measures financial status by a simple metric: *how many months of lifestyle can you afford without working?*

For Suzy, the inability to cultivate either a robust cash reserve or a proper wealth mindset created a barrier to her future success as an income investor. Though a step in the right direction, her enthusiasm for investment club principles remained too casual to pay significant dividends. Moreover, at age 37, Suzy faced the handicap of many lost wealth-building years. The aspiring *rentier* has a better statistical likelihood of reaching the necessary wealth metrics when he or she controls $75,000-$80,000 in liquid assets by age thirty.

The Low Six-Figure Hurdle

Most people who escape the Five-Figure Swamp do so with high savings and high income, a combination rare enough to ensure that beyond $100,000, the air of the wealth pyramid turns more rarified, and the halls quieter. Five-hundred million adults, out of a global population of seven billion people, claim assets worth between 100K and one million dollars. For those who started their nest eggs from scratch, without the benefit of inheritance or seed money, the achievement represents a product of toil and sacrifice.

Charlie Munger, Warren Buffet's long-time investing confidante, once famously characterized the first $100,000 as the most difficult savings hurdle. In my case, amassing the first 100K required sixteen years, from my teens to my early thirties, primarily because I gained the bulk of it from savings alone. The investments that helped fuel my later portfolio growth just didn't have much impact when I only had a few thousand, or even tens of thousands, to invest. By contrast, investment returns and higher income from my career as a communications director enabled me to gain my next 100K in four years.

At the lower echelons of the six-digit realm, the residents don't feel rich—not at all—but as $100,000 doubles and $200,000 swells still more, a curious realization sets in. The residents gain a sense of power in their relationship with money, as the ratio of savings to sacrifice turns increasingly in their favor. Where doubling $50,000 requires a decade of sacrifice, doubling $100,000 requires half the time. Yet as balance sheets expand past $300,000, the momentum, for most Americans, begins to stall. Whether because their working years come to an end, because they take on the burden of raising families and sending kids to college, or because illness, divorce, or some wealth-depriving emergency depletes their resources, the majority of American households—up to 75%--never amass assets greater than $350,000.

In some ways, 350K represents a notable number. With five times the wealth required to enter the top ten percent on a global scale, the residents of the 350K neighborhood command significant economic power. Moreover, many of those households benefit from Social Security checks that average roughly $1,300 per month. The combined cash flows from Social Security and investment income allow this cohort to sustainably generate the $32,000 per year that AARP (2016 data) lists as the average American retirement income. And while this income doesn't cover the $56,000 annual cash burn of the average American household, it does provide enough to get by—provided the retiree manages to reduce costs, budget carefully, and avoid big-ticket expenses like midnight plumbing emergencies, major automotive repairs, and wedding gifts to extended family.

A net worth that remains stuck in the low-six figure range portends a late retirement whose comfort depends on substantial infusions from Social Security or a pension. Danny, a work acquaintance who managed a team of information technology specialists, fits the profile of someone trying to surpass the low six-figure net worth hurdle. The recipient of a $130,000 per year gross salary, he claimed $200,000 in home equity, $125,000 in liquid assets (split between mutual funds and savings accounts), and annual savings between $8,000 and $10,000, or roughly ten percent of the $90,000 income left after taxes and deductions.

A Financial Services Industry Profile of a "Mass Affluent" Household	
Investable (liquid) Assets	$250,000 - $499,000
Income	$132,100
Cash Holdings	$53,600
Leverage Ratio (Debt to Assets)	43%
Likelihood of Direct Stock Ownership	29%
Age	61% are over 55
Households in Cohort	87 million
Main Financial Advisory Needs	Savings Strategies, Retirement Planning

Key financial metrics of a household with liquid investable assets between 250K & 499K (Source: John Hancock Insurance/LIMRA). Data reflect averages, effective 2016, for households in the cohort.

Accordingly, he felt "on track" financially and gave in to indulgences such as private school for his pre-teen child, an RV for weekend getaways, and a swimming pool installation. Forty years old, with a net worth just over three times his net salary, he justified this sentiment by referencing metrics promoted by certain financial literature[*]. However, "on track" meant working well into his sixties, an unfortunate projection, since in some ways Danny made a perfect Cash Craft candidate (indeed, in some ways he fit the financial services industry's profile of a "mass affluent" household). With a job yielding a top 10% salary, and financial resources convertible to a $300,000 income portfolio, he had the groundwork in place for income investing potential.

---

[*] "How Much Do I Need to Retire," Fidelity Viewpoints, 8/21/2018. The article advocates a "10X income by age 67" plan, with savings goals of 3X income by age forty, 6X by age fifty, 8X by age sixty, and 10X by age sixty-seven.

Yet a closer look at Danny's situation reveals important concerns. His low six-figure net worth stemmed from an ability to earn, not an impressive ability to save. Additionally, his propensity to acquire liabilities acted as a headwind against his assets. Subjected to an honest cost/benefit analysis, the private school tuition, RV, and swimming pool reflect wants rather than needs, expenses that disproportionately impair wealth.

In contrast to Danny, people who speedily surpass the $350,000 net worth hurdle display a few key traits:

♦ *They achieve a high savings rate*

On its own, a high income usually proves insufficient to lift the aspiring wealth builder into top levels of the wealth pyramid in a timeframe conducive to early retirement. Only the combination of high income and high savings will supply the necessary synergy—more so when supplemented with a growing dividend stream. Danny's ten percent savings rate, through traditional by historic norms and better than the national average, falls well short of rates achieved by typical early retirees, who average 30%-50% of net income in the early stages and as much as 70% in the later stages. Put another way: people who accumulate significant wealth through their own volition don't let the comfort of a steady paycheck create a false sense of complacency.

♦ *They emphasize assets and limit liabilities*

For the sake of brevity, suffice to say that assets produce cash flow, while liabilities don't. Though a simple idea on paper, the concept remains under-appreciated in real life, since people often fail to grasp the true cost of a purchase, especially purchases made with credit, and they often fail to recognize the hidden liability in things which on the surface seem valuable. Partially this tendency comes from a misguided belief that a stable, high paycheck counts as the main ingredient in financial success and provides a passport to life's finer things. In contrast, people who move quickly up the wealth pyramid regard *asset wealth*, and the passive income it supplies, as the true measure of financial success. By investment club standards, they attain $100,000 in asset wealth by age thirty-two, and $350,000 by thirty-six.

Mid-Six Figures: The Money Momentum Launchpad

The mid six-figure "launchpad," far from a metric with arbitrary significance, in fact represents an important net worth milestone. Financial planners promote the $500,000-$600,000 range as the amount of capital people close to retirement age need to purchase an annuity capable of generating a lifetime income stream equivalent to the median wage. The impatient calculus of "leanFIRE" bloggers often designates it as F-U money, a ticket out of the cubicle and into a "work optional" life. Such ideas connote an optimistic sentiment—that a net worth in the mid six figure range affords an opportunity to relax and indulge in present gratification. Committed wealth builders hold a different view. To them, a $500,000-$600,000 net worth serves as a launchpad, the basis for money momentum that, properly channeled, can propel them past seven figures in a handful of years.

A Financial Services Industry Profile of an "Affluent" Household	
Investable (liquid) Assets	$500,000 -$999,000
Income	$198,300
Cash Holdings	$87,800
Leverage Ratio (Debt to Assets)	28%
Likelihood of Direct Stock Ownership	39%
Age	69% are over 55
Households in Cohort	6.4 million
Main Financial Advisory Needs	Tax planning, Retirement Planning, Principal Growth

High income, high savings, and the deployment of that savings into income-producing assets creates a wealth synergy that places the speedy pyramid climber on the verge of real money momentum. Once experienced, this momentum provides a dose of financial confidence unknown to the global masses who crowd the lower levels of the wealth pyramid. In the neighborhood of $500,000, the residents exude a certain ebullience. Halfway to seven figures, with wealth greater than 95% of the planet, they experience savings discipline pay off in the form of higher-gear market returns. A 6% gain in their real estate or stock market assets—well within the range of historical expectations—increases their wealth by $30,000. When passive gains equate to an office clerk's annual income, the phrase "putting money to work" takes on a meaningful quality. Nearing $800,000, the residents walk with a bit of swag through the wealth pyramid's increasingly empty halls. With wealth over ten times greater than the median U.S. household, on the threshold of the global top 1%, they hear the footsteps of millionaires resonate through the ceiling above them, and easily envision the time when they too ascend to the seven-digit realm. To reach it, they need only a few good years of market returns and an ambitious savings regimen. In my case, the $500,000 I accumulated by age forty, nurtured by a synergistic combination of investment income, capital gains, and savings, doubled to a million within seven years, a money momentum inconceivable when my portfolio languished in five-figure swampland.

Pyramid climbers who achieve money momentum on this scale emphasize not only the traits necessary to advance beyond the earlier wealth tests, but also adhere to an additional perspective:

--they treat their finances as a business enterprise

In general, this means applying accounting practices to personal finance. Operational efficiency guides behavior, and forces the investor to evaluate the business of life by a ruthless rubric: *does this transaction improve or impair my finances?* Through such discipline, students of Cash Craft strive to grow a dividend stream into a dividend snowball, a source of passive income that rivals, and eventually exceeds, income derived from work. To achieve this in a reasonable timeframe, the aspiring rentier should have $500,000 in income-producing assets by age forty.

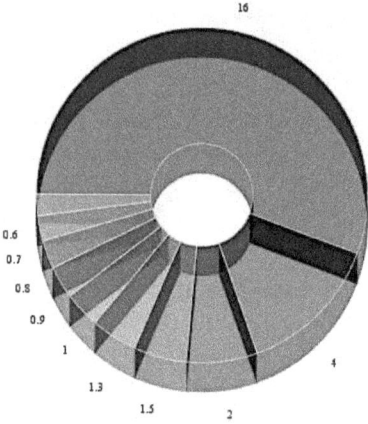

A personal portrait of money momentum, as expressed in a clockwise progression of time required to attain $1,000,000 via 100K increments. Though my first 100K required sixteen years, investment returns and higher savings rates made subsequent increments an ever-speedier achievement.

Closing Thoughts

This meditation invokes the metrics of global wealth to give Cash Craft savings philosophy some concrete reference points. Potential income investors, by asking "how much do I need to start income investing?" reduce the concept too simplistically. My discussion of the Five-Figure "Swamp," the Low-Six Figure "Hurdle," and the Mid-Six Figure "Launchpad" attempts to reframe the question as *how much do I need and by what age do I need it?* In part, I reference the wealth pyramid, and related numbers, as a rebuttal to the comparison curmudgeons. If a million dollars doesn't buy what it used to, it still represents a substantial pile of money. Those interested in pursuing a work-optional life find it offers something more robust than a token middle-finger gesture to the system. On the other hand, for people interested in greater wealth milestones, it offers a powerful dose of money momentum. An investor might conceivably retire with less, but only by entering the seven-figure net worth realm can he or she enjoy the *rentier* lifestyle in a realistically sustainable fashion.

A Financial Services Industry Profile of a "High Net Worth" Household	
Investable (liquid) Assets	$1,000,000 -$3,490,000
Income	$323,900
Cash Holdings	$195,400
Leverage Ratio (Debt to Assets)	11%
Likelihood of Direct Stock Ownership	59%
Age	77% are over 55
Households in Cohort	6 million
Main Financial Advisory Needs	Estate and trust planning, "Deep advisor relationships"

Sandwiched between the "affluent" and the "mega-millionaires," households that fit the "High Net Worth" (HNW) profile have investable liquid assets in the low seven figures range, according to the financial services industry. (Source: John Hancock Insurance/LIMRA, based on 2016 data). A stand-out data feature of the Financial Services profiles is the correlation between age and high investable wealth—the greater the liquid assets, the more likely they belong to a household aged 55+. Achieving the million-dollar portfolio thus presents the double rarity of a statistically unusual liquid net worth (a.k.a. "wet worth") at an age when, statistically, few people obtain it.

A finance guru named Penelope
Offered wealth secrets with a guarantee:
The way to manifest abundant wealth
Starts with a journey to the higher self.
"Practice gratitude and you will find
A richer dimension of the mind,"
The guru said to her eager students,
Who thought the words held wisdom and prudence.
"If you consider the journey too tough
Your sense of gratitude is not enough!"
This admonition scared her students straight--
Faithfully they began to meditate.
They read her books and they followed her blog
They attended workshops and walked her dog.
When for abundance they still tried to reach
More wisdom the guru offered to teach:
"Millionaire Secrets to Double Your Stash!"
With a discount for those who paid in cash.

--Six--

A Musing on a Campaign to Promote the Sex Appeal of Dividends

Our culture of money worship bestows a presumption of talent and wisdom on those who possess riches. Money holds such enchantment that the presumption extends even to those who project an aura of riches via glamorous façade. Rarely do people question whether having money qualifies as a barometer of talent and wisdom. I can assure them it does not, and in support of this contention offer myself as evidence. Of talent I claim no more than average and of wisdom nothing profound, other than the humility to agree with the sentiments in Woody Allen's famous aphorism, "if you want to make God laugh, tell him your plans." My *rentier* lifestyle attests more to the merits of a simple investment strategy than any personal attribute for which I deserve credit.

At cocktail parties, where giddy voices and glamorous facades contribute to an atmosphere of excitement, this modesty places me at a disadvantage, especially when acquaintances, forgetting that dividend discipline makes me averse toward trading-centered strategies, engage me in conversation about financial markets.

"What direction do you think the market will go?" they ask.
"I think it will go up and down."
"Is now a good time to buy stocks?"
"That depends on the stock," I tell them.

Disappointed by the deadpan quality of these replies, my erstwhile disciples turn, drinks in hand, to other compelling interests. As often happens at cocktail parties, these interests wear high heels and low-cut blouses which accentuate the "finer points" of human anatomy more than income investing principles. Watching my companions follow Sabrina the Venus from Valencia over to the bar, I reflect on a basic truth: dividends lack sex appeal.

From finance to fashion, sex appeal exerts a subliminal desire for excitement. I know my cocktail party companions don't really share an interest in portfolios that yield a stable 6%-7%. Rather than dividends, they seek divination, the panache of Wall Street Wizards able to conjure profits from the price-swing pendulum. Perhaps my dividend dreams make me a mediocre messenger, infusing my conversation with the meek tone of a small-ball strategist surrounded by home-run sluggers. Still, I find the brush-off irritating. Why should the Venus from Valencia arouse more excitement than a preferred stock with a 7% coupon? Can't dividends be sexy too?

In part, the problem stems from the investing world's dull vocabulary, which provides an inadequate medium for scintillating sentiments. The edgy bumper sticker humor in taglines like *golfers do it with balls* withers when couched in dry phrasings like *income investors do it with dividends*. (I suspect, however, that the much kinkier *income investors do it with cash cows* will appeal to a certain subset of the population.) Similarly, on a visual level, the investing world offers little in the way of stimulating eye candy. Charts, graphs, and financial statements make poor surrogates as objects of romantic fantasy. Though a celebrity pin-up girl might offer a remedy to such bland visuals, casting the part presents challenge. The successful dividend darling must strut between the acceptably risqué and the shamefully sleazy, a requirement that eliminates several otherwise photogenic types. Many of today's pop-culture princesses, though no doubt provocative in bikinis emblazoned with the logos of dividend-paying companies, possess neither the appropriate persona nor reputation, their names besmirched by tabloid scandal. On the other hand, today's icons of elegance—celebrities in the mold of Audrey Hepburn, Sofia Loren, or the 21st Century renditions of the type (Anne Hathaway?), sway sentiments too far in the other direction, infusing an element of snobbery into a message intended for mass appeal. In the quest for curvy yet courteous, regal yet risqué, I therefore nominate "America's Favorite Sweetheart" Sandra Bullock. With girl-next-door approachability, as stunning in a bikini as an evening gown, she makes the perfect candidate to promote the sex appeal of dividends. One pictures her posed like Christie Brinkley in a "Got Milk?" ad, only instead of smiling through a milk moustache she smiles over an annual report, while bold letters nearby convey a modified tagline: "Got Dividends?"

Cynicism about the effectiveness of a campaign to promote the sex appeal of dividends will surely keep most investors from serious involvement, even if they sympathize with the cause. I consider this unfortunate, since the campaign might produce important benefits, including:

◆*Greater free cash flow return to shareholders*: healthy companies generate more in free cash flow than they can successfully reinvest in the business. Returning the excess cash to shareholders typically proceeds via two instruments: dividends and buy-backs. Dividends put real cash in shareholder's pockets. Buy-backs project a vague possibility of capital gain into the market, under the premise that fewer shares outstanding will increase earnings per share and in turn boost the stock price. The checkered history of stock buy backs presents a cautionary tale to anyone who thinks balance sheet legerdemain translates to sustainable capital gain. Boeing's eagerness to pay $400/share during a 2018 buy-back plan can only be regarded as a destructive waste of capital in light of the $120 share price that prevailed in spring 2020. Unfortunately, such poorly timed repurchases repeatedly gain approval in America's corporate boardrooms. No shareholder ever got hurt receiving a dividend. On the other hand, as Martin Hutchinson writes in that bastion of capitalist advocacy *The National Review*, buybacks "are prone to outrageous abuse and incentivize executives to enrich themselves at shareholder expense" ("The Case against Stock Buybacks," 5/16/2020). Promoting the sex appeal of dividends—and by implication, the comparative sleaziness of buy-backs—

would pressure managers to utilize dividends as the preferred method for returning cash to shareholders.

◆*Greater honesty in accounting*: to pay a dividend, a company has to come up with real cash. While "creative accounting" might help a company disguise operational problems in the short term, no managerial shenanigans can substitute for steady cash distributions as a signifier of long-term operational health. Managers who strive for "dividend accountability" over the long-term benefit shareholders more than managers who fixate on short term "price accountability." Associating dividend accountability with sexiness could swing the spotlight of investor interest toward dividend achievers and pressure more companies to prove their mettle via steady dividend distributions.

◆*A recognition of income investors as romantic heroes*: the mythology of our culture excessively promotes bad-boy types whose square jaws and chiseled features mask troubling financial deficiencies. Too long have America's damsels suffered from financially ignorant narratives that make romantic rebels the subjects of cinematic fantasy. Let the "dividend dukes" replace these miscreants as the more enduring heroes both in our cultural mythology (not to mention the economic reality of late market capitalism). In the process, Hollywood might promote not only greater financial literacy but also role models whose "monetary masculinity" accomplishes more than fisticuffs.

As with most nascent social movements, only a few brave iconoclasts will regard this musing as a manifesto and contribute to the necessary agitation-propaganda. My plans for the cause include edgier bumper sticker humor and financial reports featuring celebrity pin up girls. God, do I hear you laughing?

--Seven--

Income Investing Beyond the Crossover Point

> *The following meditation, partially intended as a rebuttal to popular sentiments that view a "work-optional life" as an end-stage financial achievement, discusses the attributes of investors who resist "leanFIRE" dreams and eventually amass an investment income that exceeds income derived from work. Real money momentum, and its application in building a substantial dividend snowball, provides the focus of "advanced stage" money maturity.*

Time freedom—life unshackled from the demands of the working world and dedicated to the pursuit of dreams—represents the grail of those who quest for financial independence. Blessed with time freedom, the human spirit reaches heights unattainable during commute-bound existence. Roses await smelling, novels await writing, philanthropic organizations await establishment. Additionally, time freedom confers a somewhat crass but still satisfying benefit: the envious expression of cubicle-confined colleagues, who watch as you drive off into the sunset, or perhaps Napa Valley, where (presumably) you have a winery.

For those whose vision of retirement centers more on the enjoyment of wine than on practice of viniculture, and whose philanthropic ambitions fall short of commemorative plaques, the stereotypes of retirement life resemble marketing ploys more than honest assessments. Adhering to the tenets of an iconoclastic investment philosophy—income investing—I maintain an iconoclastic disregard for corporate advertising whose idealized portrayal of retirement marginalizes more personal visions.

Lee Eisenberg, in his book *The Number*, offers a humorous and insightful glimpse of how the financial planning industry packages retirement as a consumer product, intended for promotion according to the status-driven mindset of consumer culture. The status imagery of this mindset creates a powerful subliminal influence, prodding people to constantly upgrade their "numbers"—the portfolio value thought necessary for retirement bliss. Eisenberg's reportage contains a litany of people who suffer from dangling carrot syndrome, remaining on the work treadmill in an endless effort to satisfy their number-creep.

For the aspiring *rentier*, retirement propaganda offers a useful counterpoint that forces a re-examination (and hopefully re-affirmation) of personal early retirement resolve. As I write this, the internet smolders over the warning, sounded by money maven Suze Orman, that early retirees court disaster by quitting work with less than a $5 million portfolio. The assumptions (some reasonable, others outlandish) behind this admonition overlook a simple fact: a $5 million portfolio, allocated to even a conservative income approach, could sustainably generate 250K-300K per year in dividends and interest, a number so far beyond the spending needs of most people as to render it hyperbole. Clearly, neither Orman nor her leanFIRE critics have much background in the theory and practice of income investing, otherwise the controversy would never have turned into such click-bait.

Controversies such as the one inspired by Orman seem inevitable in an era when the laurels of financial expertise spread without distinction among blogosphere personalities, television celebrities, and academics. The vetting of ideas that normally occurs in an arena of reasonably informed participants succumbs, in the era of click-bait, to misinformation and the ignorance of short attention spans. Against this background, those who enter advanced-stage money maturity and behold for the first time the panorama of work-optional life may well encounter a chorus of naysayers who darken the view with shadows of doubt.

To some extent, retirement propaganda, particularly as it applies to early retirees, manages to endure because the population of those able to refute it—in particular, the population of retirees well versed in income strategies—remains statistically minimal. Given the precarious financial condition of those who occupy all but the highest levels of the wealth pyramid, early retirement, for most people, remains a theoretical concept, not a realistic idea. A legacy of debt accumulation, wage stagnation, and consumerism clouds not only the average person's financial future, but also the vocabulary by which people speak of personal finance. Today's standards of success sink so low that "financial independence"—a once venerable phrase denoting a state of wealth where investment income sustainably covers expenses—now, in popular culture, simply references a situation in which one no longer relies on credit cards or loans from the Bank of Mom and Dad.

Not surprisingly, at a time when traditional meanings fade away, a lack of clarity also surrounds the topic of work-optional living, an employment paradigm financial independence makes possible. Though the details of work-optional life vary by source, they generally share an idealized lifestyle vision founded on passion, F-U money, and disdain for the cubicle. In my view, the nuanced definitions add unnecessary complexity to a rather simple idea and reflect the efforts of early retirement bloggers to make "FIndependence Day" a cause celebre. Interestingly, while those lauded for their "FIndependence" expertise devote considerable space to the subject of the first "crossover point" (where passive income meets expenses), they give scant attention to the second— the point where passive income exceeds income derived from work.

Investors who progress toward Crossover II perceive financial independence not as a finish line but rather as a gateway toward more robust financial accomplishments. Aiming for financial abundance, not simply independence, they recognize FIRE bloggers' praise for the work-optional life as an overstatement of its virtue. Cash Craft philosophy regards "work-optionalism" simply as a state of financial independence where work follows from choice rather than need. Why choose to work, if investment income pays the bills? Those who grasp the math of money momentum can probably guess the answer: to build the dividend snowball.

Applying a Business Perspective to Personal Finance

The transition from dividend stream to dividend snowball marks the first milestone on the journey toward Crossover II. To build, in a realistic timeframe, a dividend snowball that provides investment income in excess of work income, the investor must deploy as fresh capital both the full after-tax proceeds from employment and any dividend income remaining after expenses. (This assumes the investor uses investment income to pay expenses, a practice I highly recommend.) During the initial phase of financial independence, perhaps the first two years, employment income provides the vast majority of fresh capital, as living expenses claim the lion's share of dividends. However, in the manner of a snowball, accumulating at a rate proportional to its size, the amount of dividend income in excess of expenses grows ever more rapidly, powerfully augmenting the infusion of fresh capital derived from work. Depending on a confluence of factors—amount of net employment income, the portfolio's organic dividend growth rate (from common stock dividend hikes), the ability to contain living expenses, and the average yield obtained on fresh capital—the snowball roller should achieve Crossover II in a much speedier time frame than that required to achieve initial financial independence.

If the prospect of an investment income greater than work income seems a lofty hurdle, consider that crossover metrics, properly conceived, regard work income as a *net* amount, and that tax policy bestows a more favorable treatment on money derived through passive (rather than "earned") sources. A 100K gross salary, depending on state of residency, reduces after taxes and deductions to about 70K. Put another way, an investment income of 70K roughly equates to a job paying 100K.

Income investing beyond the crossover point involves the same attributes—an ability to maintain a high savings rate, to exercise prudent risk awareness, and to acquire assets while avoiding liabilities—that enable initial crossover success. That said, investors who successfully build a dividend snowball in pursuit of

Crossover II embrace a key tendency: *they hold personal finance to the efficiency standards of a business enterprise.*

Those who manage profit-driven enterprises know the negative impact that inefficient operations and wasteful practices pose to profit margins. Yet where businesses strive to instill a mindset that grows margins and maximizes profits, most employees, as indicated by their low savings rates, engage in consumption decisions considered inefficient from a business management perspective. The investor who gains financial independence has a rare opportunity to regard a job in the same manner that owners of high margin, high cash flow enterprises regard their business: as a "cash cow." Bloggers who write about financial independence in terms of "work optionalism," and speak glowingly of finding passion and personal growth in a work-optional life, overlook the tremendous opportunity cost of quitting the cubicle. An income in the top ten percent of wage earners, and the high savings rate that income allows, doesn't mean less when other sources pay the bills. Rather, it becomes more valuable, for it allows money momentum on a scale previously unattainable.

Considering a job as a "cash cow" may seem counter-intuitive to those whose early retirement motivation entails dreams of stepping away from the hours-for-dollars treadmill. If so, a consideration of the counter-intuitive manner in which Warren Buffet built the Berkshire Hathaway holding company may prove instructive. In his biography of Buffet, Roger Lowenstein details how the sage investor began acquiring shares of Berkshire—at the time a textile manufacturer—during the 1960s, a period of significant decline for the American textile industry. Where the financial world saw a business threatened by increasing foreign competition, Buffet saw opportunity—not in textiles, but in the seed-corn potential of Berkshire's free cash flow. Upon gaining control of the company, Buffet told his managers to abandon their efforts to grow or improve the business. The sage investor then redeployed all profit (beyond the minimum necessary to continue basic production) as fresh capital in other ventures (Coca-Cola, GEICO, etc.) that fit his rubric for long term returns. In essence,

Buffet milked the Berkshire cash cow, turning the free cash flow of its stagnant operations into seed money for a new, diversified asset base. The Berkshire example offers a template for personal finance. Though the financially independent investor may well view cubicle life as a declining enterprise unworthy of "reinvestment," the free cash flow provided by the operation offers tremendous potential as seed money for the holding company known as the investment portfolio.

Case History: A Job as a Cash-Cow Enterprise

Andre, an investment club member whose blue-collar manufacturing experience stood in contrast to the other members' white-collar resumes, provides a lesson in how cash-cow thinking can apply to the workplace. Working his way up from machinist to foreman at a metal shop that serviced L.A.'s maritime industry, Andre gleaned a sense of management expertise, and developed aspirations beyond the shop floor. When the shop owner decided to retire, Andre bought the business. For a few years, things went well, until new robotic technology brought game-changing disruption to machine shop economics. To stay competitive, Andre realized he had to upgrade the shop's increasingly obsolete equipment, a capital-intensive process that threw a monkey wrench into the anticipated profit forecast. Fortunately, a shop down the street, seeking the legacy business of Andre's customer base, offered to buy him out, with the caveat that Andre return to his old job as foreman. Happy to let someone else shoulder the burden of adapting to a changing industry, Andre accepted.

"In the machine-shop business we have a saying," Andre recalled. "You're either *in the business* or *on the business*. *In the business* means working hard, sweating over deadlines and deliveries, and stressing about delinquent accounts receivable. *On the business* means the shop runs itself, for the most part, allowing free time for other pursuits, such as my real passion—restoring classic cars. I thought buying the shop would put me *on* the business. Instead it put me more *in* the business than ever." Regarding the subject of financial independence, Andre provided a humble perspective: "looking back on it, I got extremely lucky that someone came along to bail me out. In truth, I couldn't afford business ownership; it left me no margin for error."

As an employee, Andre actually enjoyed a basic level of financial independence. He had a paid-off house and a decent chunk of savings. Financing the purchase of the shop, and later, the prospect of financing equipment upgrades, put that in jeopardy. Thankfully, he sold at a profit, restoring his earlier finances. Meanwhile, he perceived his old role as shop foreman in a whole new light. His capital needs were minimal, his overhead expenses practically nonexistent. Though a return to the shop floor meant his top-line numbers took a hit, his operating margins—income received minus the cost of obtaining it—improved to the point that he made similar money per unit of time. Burning his hands on the stove of business ownership, with its attendant hazards of purchase order financing, equipment upgrades, and regulatory expenses, taught Andre what a sweet gig he enjoyed as a decently paid worker. *"In the money game, the certainty of a decent income stream that costs little to maintain beats the possibility of high income that costs a lot to maintain,"* he emphasized.

Highly successful entrepreneurs may disagree with Andre's sentiments, but I find an important lesson in the anecdote. Applying a business framework to personal finance forces the wealth builder to judge monetary decisions by a ruthless yet elegantly simple standard: *does this transaction improve or degrade my finances?* Since transactions sometimes prove beneficial or harmful only in hindsight, the standard involves a degree of estimation. The concepts of *margin for error* and *risk adjusted return* help to keep estimates within objective parameters. Basically, margin for error frames a transaction in terms of affordability: what consequences arise if things go wrong? Risk adjusted return frames a transaction in normative terms: given alternatives, does it represent a wise course of action?

Ideally, a transaction fits positively in both frameworks, but in practice people often ignore one or the other. A single lottery ticket, for example, fits well in the affordability framework, its marginal cost only a minimal threat to a responsible player's finances. However, given the extremely low odds of winning, plus the fact that the aggregate capital committed to lottery tickets could achieve better productivity elsewhere, the purchase offers terrible risk-adjusted return. Measured by actual numbers, Andre's decision to trade a job for entrepreneurial adventure fails the test of risk-adjusted return. Though he sold the business for a 100K profit—a 20% gain on the 500K purchase price—it took him five years to do so, meaning he achieved a mere 4% return on an annualized basis. Considering that Andre took on substantial risk (not to mention the headaches and long hours of active management) to achieve a result less than the historic average of the stock market, we realize how his foray into entrepreneurial life lacked appreciation for risk-adjusted return. Ironically, had Andre applied business principles to his personal finances, he would likely have avoided going into business in the first place. Assessing the transaction in terms of its likelihood to improve or diminish his finances, he would have better anticipated pitfalls in the entrepreneurial path.

Appreciating a job as a cash-cow enterprise serves as a key trait of those who grow a dividend stream into a dividend snowball. Until Crossover II—the point where investment income exceeds work income—a job likely represents the highest income per input of time and cost that an investor can reasonably achieve. To the extent that business accounting principles benefit personal finance, the concepts of margin-for-error and risk-adjusted return help build a foundation for "snowball success." In addition, the following traits, gleaned from my investment club colleagues who held forth on the subject, offer a general sense of appropriate habits:

♦ "You use investment income to pay expenses"—Charles R., (retired at 50, portfolio value 1.8 million)

According to Charles, income investing beyond the crossover point means containing costs as well as building the dividend snowball: *"Savings rate and income growth represent flipsides of the same financial coin;*

success in the former helps fuel the latter. Paying expenses with dividends—swept each month into a checking account through an automated ACH process—provides a mental reinforcement of lifestyle affordability, meaning you can sustain a lifestyle from dividends alone. Though the ACH may make a money-go-round of cash flows—your brokerage receives infusions of paycheck cash only to regurgitate dividend cash, it creates a two-fold practical benefit. First, it encourages a portfolio designed for the production of predictable monthly cash. Since bills accrue on a monthly basis, it only makes sense that monthly ACH distributions cover them. Second, the practice makes the emotional transition to post-paycheck life much easier. We spend so much of our lives working to pay bills that the prospect of another approach seems almost mythical. Seeing it work in practice goes a long way to boosting retirement confidence."

◆ "You take measures to protect wealth from misfortune"—Clifton P. (retired at 52, portfolio value 2.3 million)

To Clifton, the accumulation of assets sufficient to confer financial independence also places the investor on the cusp of deep pockets status. *"Snowball stage investors often express surprise upon learning that their assets exceed the liability limit of the standard auto insurance policy. However, the list of possible misfortunes extends well beyond those encountered on the road. At the very least, the investor at this stage of money maturity should consider purchasing an umbrella policy that offers coverage not only for physical damages but also wonton civil claims. Investors with an entrepreneurial side-gig should take measures to shield personal assets from those affiliated with the venture. Finally, if involved in a romantic relationship likely to result in marriage, the investor should insist on a pre-nuptial agreement. Though uncomfortable, the pre-nup conversation can shed light on the often-unstated financial assumptions relationships entail. At its essence, marriage is a legal contract with financial implications, from which a pre-nuptial agreement can provide a measure of insulation."*

◆ "You produce quarterly and annual financial statements and make an annual projection of growth"—Candace L., (retired at 45, portfolio value 2.5 million)

Candace attributes a practical a philosophical purpose to such paperwork: *"Unless your cash flow derives from highly unusual sources, financial independence will likely entail a stream of unearned income that creates a quarterly estimated tax liability. A detailed tally of investment income, broken down according to tax-exempt interest, non-dividend distributions, qualified dividends, and ordinary dividends, will help you not only anticipate this liability but also sense trends in the nature of portfolio cash flows—for example, whether tax-advantaged income comprises an efficient portion of the total. If this seems tedious, or something better outsourced to an accountant, consider that successful business owners keep detailed inventories of their assets and the nature of the cash flows those assets produce. Similarly, a detailed tally of expenses— rent/mortgage, utilities, food, transportation, entertainment, and incidentals— helps gauge trends in numbers that, according to a business mindset, you might regard as 'operating costs' in your personal financial enterprise."*

To Candace, the production of quarterly reports allows a holistic financial assessment, with improvement denoted by a growing income relative to operating costs. Candace advocated using a comparison of sequential financial assessments to project a realistic target for income growth: *"Using 'Rule of 72' metrics, and assuming annual investment income growth in the 7% to 10% range, the snowball roller could expect to double income in approximately eight years. Investors who utilize a 50% savings rate—a common savings rate target for early retirees—to achieve Crossover I will require an investment income double that for Crossover II. Assuming conservative portfolio value and yield recommendations, the investor who achieved financial independence with an annual investment income of 36K, a 6% yield on a 600K portfolio, requires 72K, the product of a 1.2 million portfolio yielding an average of 6%, to achieve Crossover II."*

◆ "You maximize investment strategies that produce up-front cash"—Ruben J. (retired at 55, portfolio value 2 million)

Though Ruben regularly sang the praises of CEFs and attributed his Crossover II success to his 100% CEF portfolio, he went on to explain his comment with an intriguing theoretical exercise concerning preferred stock: *"For the snowball roller, a high but stagnant yield will beat low but growing yield. I've charted this out several times, using different yield and growth numbers, but offer the following scenario for simplicity. The nominal dollars paid by an equity ETF with a 2.5% yield and an 8% annualized dividend growth rate (SCHD, let's say) take around twenty-four years to equal the nominal dollars paid by 7% coupon preferred. By 'nominal dollars' I mean total cash received. Let's assume a 100k allocation to each security. The nominal-dollar crossover point happens in Year Twenty-four, when the total income delivered by the ETF (almost 183K) will surpass the total income delivered by the preferred (175K). Now, I realize that defenders of dividend growth will claim they care less about total cash received than the point when the ETF provides a higher payout than the preferred. I've charted this too; such a crossover takes nearly fifteen years—the cash payout from a 2.5% yield growing by 8% annually will surpass a 7% preferred in Year 15. But this metric ignores the opportunity cost of disregarding total income. Assuming an investment of 100K in each security, the total cash flow received over fifteen years will be about 68K for the ETF and 105K for the preferred, a 37K difference, or 50% more money, in favor of the preferred. And keep in mind, these numbers assume a fairly optimistic dividend growth clip of 8% for the ETF. How many securities do that for fifteen years, let alone twenty-five? Very few... certainly not enough for the snowball roller to justify sacrificing up-front cash for a dividend growth ETF approach."*

Among the many ideas gleaned during my affiliation with the investment club, Ruben's point about the significance of nominal high yield cash flows remains one of the most intriguing, presenting a perspective rarely discussed in the financial independence blogosphere.

The Time Value of Time

The concept of Crossover II deserves emphasis for a reason: it opens a more emphatic gateway to work-optional life than mere financial independence. Only when investment income exceeds work income can the investor scrutinize employment according to an objective, unemotional cost-benefit analysis. The knowledge that, on an annual (if not monthly) basis, one gains more income from assets than from work allows a fuller appreciation of time. The appreciation of the present that leads the financier to posit the "time value of money"—the idea that present dollars offer more value than future dollars—in similar fashion compels the budding *rentier* to perceive the "time value of time," a perception which foregrounds passionate living over monetary gain.

Those who appreciate the "time value of time" approach early retirement with determination and purpose. Apart from this philosophical benefit, Crossover II offers a powerful financial benefit, effectively placing the investor on the doorstep of financial abundance. An investor whose passive income exceeds the net income from a top 10% salary, and who deploys the entirety of his/her free cash flow as fresh capital, will achieve financial abundance (a passive income of 100K+) very quickly—perhaps in a handful of years. In practical terms, assuming prudent portfolio management and a robust cash reserve, it requires an investment portfolio of roughly 1.5 to 2 million dollars.

The transition from financial freedom to financial abundance marks the final milestone of Cash Craft money maturity. By linking abundance to a specific metric—early retirement on a passive income of 100K—the philosophy offers the aspiring *rentier* a guidepost for progress. That said, those of us who assemble from scratch an investment portfolio that sustainably produces an annual six-figure income, and understand how financial insight prods insight into other life concerns, know that successful progress through this level of money maturity leads not to a finish line, but rather the beginnings of a bigger journey, one measured less by monetary milestones than by personal and spiritual growth.

A culture of money worship will no doubt regard such sentiments as "sappy," perhaps because a culture given to money worship associates wealth with power and measures achievement in status terms. As a counterpoint, my investment club mentors offered insight worth pondering. Ultimately, they contended, wealth amounts to a socially constructed concept that, paradoxically, confers the benefit of escape from social structures. The universe doesn't care how much money you have in the bank, or what kind of car you drive, or which social functions you attend. However, the miracle of our existence, and the beautiful mystery it confronts us with, suggests that the universe wants us to live interesting, meaningful, adventurous lives. A *rentier* existence represents an audacious achievement—but in the end an achievement less important than the lifestyle *choices* financial abundance makes possible.

During my association with the investment club, I gleaned few specifics about the lifestyle details of a financially abundant life. Club expertise focused on the achievement of financial abundance, not its moral or philosophical implications. However, through subtle messaging conveyed in offhand conversation and in the example of their lives, my colleagues hinted that financial abundance, applied without restraint to the "gaudy bauble" of consumer culture, achieved nothing interesting, meaningful, or adventurous.

In the interest of full disclosure, I should comment on the role that the promise of a pension played in my own journey to financial abundance. I could not have achieved early retirement funded by 100K in passive income without the inclusion, in my asset column, of a defined-benefit pension that replaced 40% of my pay. This pension, with its 2% annual COLA increase, offered significant implications for my investment strategy. Instead of striving to roll a dividend snowball into six figures, I could relax somewhat, knowing my portfolio needed to produce "only" 60K. Additionally, the guarantee of an annual 2% COLA allowed me to take a more inflation-agnostic stance toward asset allocation, such that I place a relatively greater emphasis on high current income and a relatively lower emphasis on future income growth. Effectively, this means I overweight high yield, slow growth equities and REITs, leveraged fixed income CEFs, preferred stocks, etc.—securities that lift my average weighted portfolio yield into the 6% to 7% range. Finally, when calculated according to standard conversion formulas (based on prevailing treasury note yields), this pension adds roughly 1.3 million dollars in net worth equivalence to my asset column, a boon that strengthens my psychological tolerance for the occasional red ink spilled on my balance sheet by market swoons.

On occasion, during conversations with people curious about my income investing philosophy, the news that I possess such a pension leads to cynical accusations, as though I've hidden in fine print the secret sauce of my finances. In response, I generally point out that only a few of my investment club colleagues had recourse to a pension similar to mine. Most club members, after careers in the private sector, looked forward to a comparatively humbler combination of social security and IRA withdrawals as supplemental income streams—supplements that required much higher minimum age eligibility. Yet these club members typically adopted investing approaches even more aggressive than mine, achieving average portfolio yields in the 8%-9% range. Ruben, a club member who worked for decades as a fixed income analyst for an insurance company, ran a $2 million portfolio consisting entirely of closed-end bond funds yielding 9%-11%, and consistently generated 200K in annual investment income. Put another way: if possession of a robust pension provides an income investing shortcut, the lack of such a pension in no way precludes prospective *incomistas* from attaining cash craft success.

That said, a defined-benefit pension proved so consequential to my retirement—lifting me through Crossover II and into the doorway of financial abundance—that it merits some discussion, potentially in light of the popular interest in early retirement. First, to indulge in a bit of social commentary, I suspect a correlation exists between the increasing interest in "leanFIRE" and the private sector's increasing preference for *defined contribution* (rather than defined benefit) retirement plans. When a retirement plan depends solely on contributions and market gains, rather than a guaranteed lifetime income stream, the incentive to put in twenty-plus years at a job diminishes considerably. While other insecurities and frustrations cloud the cubicle, cynicism for the defined-contribution model probably ranks high among them. (For further information on the divisive history of pension politics, and trends that make the defined-benefit model nearly extinct in the private sector yet an enduring perquisite in the public sector, I recommend Roger Lowenstein's *While America Aged*.) Second, to offer some unsolicited advice, I recommend the young career seeker take heed and weigh job opportunities not merely by the glitter of high immediate pay. Though its value grows slowly and to little fanfare, a defined-benefit pension can add literally millions of dollars in deferred compensation and deliver a lifetime income stream whose total far exceeds the amount contributed via paycheck deduction.

Elsewhere I stated that I wrote this book for a target audience similar to me at age forty: established career, salary nudging into six figures, and investments around 500K. This audience, for whom the siren song of leanFIRE resonates with particular force, stands to gain particular benefit from "cash craft" money milestones. The final milestone of money maturity—the transition from financial freedom to financial abundance—represents nothing more than cash flow transformed by the catalyst of time and good money habits. Assuming adherence to such habits, and a willingness to let the catalyst do its work, the investor can, with a final effort at delayed gratification, replace leanFIRE dreams with "fatFIRE" plans. Though the details of these plans may require a consideration of matters beyond the scope of this book, I suspect that 100K in annual passive income will go a long way toward their fulfillment.

*With designer suits and a Mercedes
Marvin could really impress the ladies
Impeccable taste and a style to match
Made the man seem like a consummate catch—
His dating profile won admiration
Of hopeful singles across the nation.
But behind the façade he wore a frown—
His portfolio kept dwindling down;
The nightlife that gave him so much pleasure
Cost a disturbing amount of treasure.
So, a wealth advisor he then did hire
To help him balance spending and desire.
The advisor gave him some tough advice:
"Your suits look snazzy and your car looks nice,
But you don't need style and a Mercedes
To make an impression on the ladies.
Real women express an affinity
For monetary masculinity!"
Yet while Marvin gave the idea some praise
He did not fully understand the phrase.
And so his portfolio dwindled down—
But he enjoyed some great nights on the town.*

--Eight--

A Meditation on Non-Numeric Measures of Net Worth

Do net worth assessments based on the standard metric of assets minus liabilities overlook important variables? Written in 2018, the following meditation examines unconventional net worth assessments and considers their potential to provide a more holistic picture of personal wealth.

The investment club used the phrase "Pecuniary Paradox" to reference an ironic feature of money-- that in a world of abundant wealth, there remains a scarcity of wealthy*.

Self-made millionaires with unconventional views, they often took exception to the financial media, and reacted with displeasure to personal finance articles portraying a million dollars as an anemic amount. Noting how the same cost of living increases that erode wealth also erode the ability to attain it, the club wondered if the personal finance authors actually possessed the million dollars their articles disparaged. When club sentiments turned self-righteous, Charles, a club member whose banking background made him more amenable to mainstream finance, advised tolerance of views that ran counter to investment club sentiment. "You don't have to be a mechanic to write insightfully about cars,"

---

* Current statistics continue the trend noted twenty years ago by scholars Stanley and Danko, who asserted in the *Millionaire Next Door* "there has never been more personal wealth in America than there is today. . .yet most Americans are not wealthy. Nearly one-half of our wealth is owned by 3.5% of our households. Most of the other households don't even come close."

he cautioned. "Before you critique the media, remember that our own views could invite derision from people whose riches exceed ours."

Charles's comment reminds me to apply relativism my own situation, and to leave open the question of what confers authority in matters of finance. As a resident not of the penthouse, but rather the wealth pyramid's less-exclusive top floor, I admit my own credentials lack a sterling quality. Yet we live in a world of relative circumstance, and if we admit for exhibit only those reports from the extremes of experience—the wealthiest investors, the most famous celebrities, the most learned scholars—our awareness remains incomplete. Placing my million-dollar journey in the context of global wealth implies a recognition of its relative significance. In fact, a consideration of net worth on relativistic terms reveals interesting facets otherwise unseen.

Considering the Million Dollar Portfolio in Relativistic Terms

Income investing encourages a perspective of net worth measured not by numerical value alone, but by the same metrics applied to corporations, income securities, and private investment opportunities. Just as companies with similar market capitalizations might carry different investment grades and liquidation values, so too might individuals with similar net-worth numbers rank differently depending on the allocation of their assets. Measuring net worth by the traditional method—the sum of assets minus liabilities—produces an incomplete picture, because numerical value, on its own, says nothing about quality and productivity. A million dollars, in other words, requires subjective assessment as a combination of asset choices and income potential.

An income portfolio manager might regard high quality assets as those which provide stability of principal, regular cash flow, and liquidity. Assets ranked as low quality, unsurprisingly, demonstrate the opposite—uncertainty of principal, erratic cash flow, and extreme illiquidity. Between these extremes, quality ranking depends on an interplay of positive and negative factors. An asset might not provide principal stability, but still offer the benefits of reliable cash flow growth and high liquidity (blue-chip stocks, for example). For investors, quality describes the likelihood of an asset to safeguard capital in "real" terms—net of inflation—such that it maintains future purchasing power.

The investing public often translates "safeguard" as "maintain stable price," but experienced investors recognize the oversimplification in that view. If price stability counted as the chief feature of asset quality, then a Mason jar stuffed with cash and hidden in a secret place would rank as a quality asset. The fact that even the most conservative professional money managers don't build portfolios around Mason jars suggests that investors weigh price stability in the context of a bigger consideration: the need to find a return *on* capital as much as a return *of* capital. Where these drives intersect—essentially, the locus of productivity and quality—we find a judgement about asset rank.

The Quality/Productivity Rubric

Extrapolating this rubric to the realm of personal finance, the investment club surmised that numerically similar net worth values might merit quite different relative ranks. Millionaire "A," whose net worth consists entirely of equity in personal residential property, might possess quality with little productivity, while Millionaire "B," with wealth deployed in a diversified basket of income-producing securities—dividend stocks, REITs, bonds, MLPs, etc.—enjoys both quality and productivity. Millionaire "B," generating passive cash flow from wealth allocated to liquid publicly traded securities, merits a higher relative rank than Millionaire "A," whose wealth generates no cash flow, requires months to liquidate, and incurs liabilities in the form of insurance, bills, repairs, and taxes. Productive wealth deserves a higher relative rank than non-productive wealth, though both might represent identical numeric values.

Ranking net worth in terms of quality requires a consideration of the way wealth reacts to shock. A millionaire whose net worth depends on the market price of volatile "growth" stocks might, in the event of a significant market swoon, lose a digit from his/her credentials, while the millionaire with a diversified income portfolio retains seven-figure status.

Howard Marks, the well-regarded co-founder of Oaktree Capital Management, discusses in his 2011 book The Most Important Thing how asset quality can create relatively different values from numerically similar amounts: *"$10 million earned through Russian roulette does not have the same value as $10 million earned through the diligent and artful practice of dentistry. They are the same, can buy the same goods, except that one's dependence on randomness is greater than the other. To your accountant, though, they would be identical. . .Yet, deep down, I cannot help but consider them as qualitatively different."*

In 2018, the markets provided an acute display of randomness, with the tech-heavy NASDAQ declining 25% from its highs. Million-dollar portfolios heavily weighted to the index suffered losses in the hundreds of thousands. By contrast, my diversified income portfolio weathered the same market swoon with a garden-variety haircut of 4%. Though I watched tens of thousands evaporate from my net worth, I never suffered eviction from the Realm of Seven Figures. Moreover, my portfolio's productivity, built around cash flow rather than market price, continued in full gear, and increased into 2019, bolstered by dividend boosts and—thanks to my cash reserve—the purchase of securities at depressed prices. By investment club standards, the resilience of my portfolio in the face of a significant market swoon merits higher relative net worth rank than one which, at the 2018 market highs, attained similar numeric value but later demonstrated greater fragility.

The Lens of Personal Potential

The quality/productivity rubric provides one lens by which we can regard a million dollars beyond its numeric value. Another lens, which the investment club termed "Personal Potential," encourages a view of wealth in the context of its relationship to the wealth-holder. Factors such as life circumstance, temperament, and receptivity to wealth's transformational benefits influence an individual's personal potential.

Regarding personal potential as "character" limits the concept too narrowly. While a million dollars managed by someone of good character deserves a higher ranking than a million dollars managed by a rogue, the tendency of millionaires to outsource wealth management to licensed advisors means the concept of personal character must encompass more than stewardship capability. Life circumstances also pay a role. Seen through the lens of personal potential, a million dollars at thirty-five carries more impact than at sixty-five. The young millionaire, whose robust health and sense of adventure enable a greater range of activity, extracts more joy per unit of spending. The assumption here relies on analogy: quality of life matters to the wealth-holder the way asset quality matters to a portfolio.

Admittedly, quality of life assessments invite subjectivity, a subjectivity amplified further when we seek to measure the transformational effect of wealth on the possessor. Though a homeless person in sudden possession of a million-dollar lottery ticket will exhibit an obvious material transformation arising from the newfound riches, in the more common and realistic situation of the self-made millionaire, especially one who gains wealth by adhering to an income investing regimen, the transformation likely manifests inwardly and psychologically rather than through outward materialism. The wise self-made millionaire, knowing that the habits which produce wealth also assist in preserving it, continues a six-digit lifestyle even after establishing seven-digit credentials. The true blessing of wealth manifests not so much as an abundance of money but as an abundance of time—more particularly, time freedom, the opportunity to explore existence according to personal preference.

Though a quest for time underlies most early retirement dreams, I wonder if most early retirees, especially those eager for leanFIRE, recognize the implications of time freedom for personal potential. The conventional view of retirement—one promoted in the advertisements of financial services companies—regards life after work as a pleasure pursuit. The emotional appeal in this portrayal conceals the limitation. Cash Craft philosophy presents time freedom as an opportunity to live creatively, expressing the audacity of a *rentier* lifestyle. Through the lens of personal potential, this might translate as an ability to extract creativity from a given unit of time. Another transformative realization might center on concepts of self. Residing in the seven-figure realm, living a work-optional life, the enlightened *rentier* may well dismiss notions of identity that link social-status to job title. The tendency of people to let occupation center their sense of identity may strike those blessed with financial freedom as a form of cultural brainwashing, for which the inevitable cocktail-party interrogative "what do you do?" provides subtle reinforcement. The more meaningful question, to those interested in non-occupational sources of identity, might investigate something entirely different: *"what do you dream?"*

I posit that financial freedom means little if we remain tethered to conventional financial aspirations. Unfortunately, the messages perpetuated by our status-driven culture on both an overt and subliminal level make cultivating a non-occupational sense of identity an act of iconoclasm difficult to embrace. After all, the status conferred by profession or career title, and affirmed by commensurate pay grades, represents the outward manifestation of a competition mindset encouraged since childhood. Unless guided by strong teaching to the contrary, we learn from an early age to perceive *getting* as a form of *winning* and to bestow prestige upon those who demonstrate a talent for accumulation. Too often, our jobs and careers provide an outlet for the expression of our core occupational identity, that of getters and accumulators. Because we associate accumulation with security, untethering ourselves from the occupational mindset that seems to produce security proves psychologically challenging.

In the area of personal potential, a willingness to discard the psychological baggage of accumulative thinking offers perhaps the greatest catalyst for transformation. Contrary to popular culture, which sees the attainment of a seven-figure portfolio as "victory" in the money game, I contend that the sense of security which our consumer culture grants to successful accumulators cannot in itself offer meaningful satisfaction. With unfortunate frequency, the "getting equals winning" mentality produces millionaires whose values reinforce a "culture of me." Me-ness, as a psychological and behavioral paradigm, provides a poor framework for growth, insight, or transformation.

I anticipate some readers may regard the above statement as unsolicited moralizing open to a few noteworthy rebuttals. First, social Darwinists might argue that an accumulation mindset merely represents a survival response to a predatory, hostile world, where failure to stockpile resources usually betokens future misery, a socially unattractive prospect. In this view, a strategy that promotes survival deserves commendation more than critique. Second, to voice the sentiments of economists and politicians amenable to the legacy of Adam Smith, unabashed personal indulgence, combined with the animal spirits of capitalism, benefits not just the consumer but also those who supply goods and services. The message: spending helps the economy, and the pursuit of pleasure encourages people to spend.

Whatever its justification, the me-centered life perpetuates a fundamentally uninteresting narrative. Magnifying through wealth the behavioral tendencies of consumer-culture treadmill achievers accomplishes nothing particularly noteworthy or inspirational. On the other hand, using wealth to foreground creativity and community over consumption and competition offers a framework for a more transformative experience. The lens of personal potential regards the millionaire who deploys wealth toward inspirational projects as worthy of a higher net worth ranking than the millionaire interested in selfish, insular joy.

To help clarify the attributes of an "inspirational project," I offer the following criteria: 1) it offers enjoyment, 2) it benefits others, and 3) *you do it for free*. Some jobs, many careers, and a wide range of artistic performance meet the first two tests, insofar as they render service or entertainment. The third criterion lifts the bar to a much higher standard and invokes the question, *to what extent do we truly do things for free?* The RV vacationer whose window sticker proudly displays membership in the "Good Sam Club" might, without thought of personal gain, pull over to assist a stranded motorist, if the kindness doesn't involve substantial inconvenience, such as a lengthy detour. By contrast, the RV vacationer who voluntarily patrols the nation's highways for the specific purpose of assisting strangers in need raises Samaritanism to an amazingly inspirational level.

The idea that wealth means more when directed toward a community benefit carries a long history. Readers familiar with religious aphorisms may recognize it as the biblical sentiment expressed in Luke 12:48: "for unto whomsoever much is given, of him shall much be required." Prior to Christianity, ancient Greeks considered duty as *choregoi* an honorable function whereby wealthy citizens enhanced the culture of the city-state by funding theatrical productions. The echoes of this historical and philosophical legacy resonate only faintly in our me-centered society where gated housing enclaves project exclusivity rather than community. People who after years of toil find themselves able to purchase an address in such enclaves may well feel a sense of entitlement that exclusivity helps reinforce. Countering this psychology, Cash Craft philosophy offers a simple admonition: the true measure of wealth lies not in things but in time freedom. To how much time can we consider ourselves entitled? Does passing it in an exclusive enclave really imbue it with greater meaning?

The Political Lens

This meditation considers asset choice and personal potential as contexts for exploring the significance of a million dollars beyond its numeric value. Economists, sociologists, and other scholars will no doubt look for a greater consideration of its political significance. I hesitate to invoke politics, because I consider it a theoretical distraction largely extraneous to the successful practice of income investing. Human history provides little evidence that any political system has ever produced *substantial* wealth for a substantial portion of a given population. Political solutions to the problem of financial inequality result at best in marginal improvements. Additionally, income investing entails the cultivation of a financial philosophy that no political party particularly endorses and consequently no politician fully supports. Today's politics twist conversations of financial inequality around myths that perpetuate inaccurate views of asset wealth. Those who advocate "hard work and family values" as a path to wealth ignore the fact that the world abounds with poor people who work hard and care for their families yet find even minimum levels of wealth beyond reach. In truth, hard work and upstanding values lead to wealth only if the worker has the opportunity to transform labor into capital and put that capital to productive use. Similarly, social activists ignore statistics when they bemoan the link between wealth and privilege. Statistics show that the majority of wealthy families squander their money over the course of a few generations, an indication that wealth mindsets do not arise automatically from proximity to money but instead require cultivation. Inheritance and networks of social connection provide advantage only if the beneficiary understands the difference between wealth and riches. Moreover, studies of millionaires indicate that, among those who attain wealth, determination and good money habits stand out as the true common denominators*.

The fact that individuals have attained wealth in all political systems and through all periods of recorded history (both in times of order and upheaval) suggests that personal money consciousness plays the decisive role in asset acquisition, regardless of the external political climate. This observation may irk both the challengers and defenders of the status quo. As a self-made millionaire who began transforming labor into capital while still a teenager working

---

* In a November 2018 online article, "7 Myths about Millionaires," published by *US News and World Report*, Tom Sightings references a study by Fidelity Investments that reports up to 88% of millionaires are self-made.

for minimum wage, I find the observation worth pondering. Though society might argue over which legislative tweaks make the "system" operate better, I highly doubt if any solution will compel the *en masse* transformation of labor into capital, and the skillful deployment of that capital to productive use, capable of launching large numbers of people into comfortable early retirement. The early retiree living off interest and dividends will likely always present an economic, social, and political curiosity.

Those who study money and its distribution often come to see net worth as a barometer of underlying social factors that, collectively, enhance or inhibit the ability of people to acquire wealth. Inevitably, the political lens correlates wealth with privilege and poverty with hardship. Children who grow up amid the emotional turmoil of broken families, the influence of criminogenic neighborhoods, and the intimidation of racial bias often never get a chance to join the rat race, let alone amass assets necessary for escape velocity. There is also the sobering observation presented in *Nickel and Dimed*, Barbara Ehrenreich's classic expose of wage slave life, that millions of Americans, regardless of the circumstances of their upbringing, do not earn a living wage. When anemic earnings force workers to choose between buying food or paying rent, a form of degradation that involves corporate (and by extension, investor) complicity, political arguments deserve consideration. As Ehrenreich writes in the final chapter of *Nickel and Dimed*:

> *Most civilized nations compensate for the inadequacy of wages by providing relatively generous public services such as health insurance, free or subsidized childcare, subsidized housing, and effective public transportation. But the United States, for all its wealth, leaves its citizens to fend for themselves—facing market-based rents, for example, on their wages alone. . .It is common, among the non-poor, to think of poverty as a sustainable condition—austere perhaps, but they do get by, don't they? What is harder for the nonpoor to see is poverty as acute distress: the lunch that consists of Doritos or hot dog rolls, leading to faintness before the end of the shift. The "house" that is also a car or a van. The illness or injury that must be worked*

through with gritted teeth because there's no sick pay or health insurance and the loss of one day's pay will mean no groceries for the next. These experiences are not part of a sustainable lifestyle, even a lifestyle of chronic deprivation and relentless low-level punishment. They are, by almost any standard of subsistence, emergency situations. And that is how we should see the poverty of so many millions of low wage Americans—as a state of emergency.

I sympathize with the progressive social welfare arguments that arise from this observation, though such sentiments may seem heretical to the traditional capitalist narrative that regards a million dollars as the deserved product of hard work and smarts. My own million-dollar journey convinces me that the traditional capitalist narrative tells only half the story. While hard work and smarts figured prominently in my first 500K—and especially the first 100K—I rode to millionaire status on the back of investment income and capital gains. Put another way, where investment returns accounted, on average, for maybe twenty-five percent of my first 500K, they accounted for roughly sixty-five percent of the next.

Cumulatively, averaged through the years, dividends and capital gains contributed roughly 45% of my net worth. I can't take personal credit for wealth resulting from market dynamics beyond my control. Of course, those who earn millionaire status through entrepreneurship alone, or years of creative toil that suddenly pay off—an obscure writer who suddenly tops the bestseller list, for example, or an inventor who finally builds a better mouse trap after years of tinkering—likely hold a different view. My capitalist critique doesn't devalue the animal spirits of those who win the economic lottery. Rather, it suggests that the traditional narrative downplays the role of money momentum in wealth creation. Money momentum magnifies the result of hard work in a way unimaginable to those who work hard but lack assets.

"I had found that money is like a sixth sense without which you could not make use of the other five."

—W Somerset Maugham

--Nine--

A Meditation on Savings as the Foundation of Wealth

Observing that capitalism benefits most those who possess capital, the following meditation explores the psychological traits which encourage the perception of cash as an asset. Written in 2018, nine years into a period of low interest rates that made savings accounts a red-headed stepchild to the siren song of stocks, it offers a reminder that cash savings—in particular, the productive potential represented by cash savings—remains valuable in all stages of the money game. The cultivation of a robust savings mentality, perhaps the most foundational money habit, lies at the core of the wealth building process.

In America, a country which cherishes individual freedom as a birthright, dependency on others for economic security proves particularly stressful. When a job provides the primary (or often, the only) source of income, words like "freedom" quickly reduce to empty rhetoric. For the sake of a job, people will submit to unspeakable degradations, compromise moral standards, and sacrifice dreams. On a subsistence level, a job represents food and shelter. On a psychological level, it represents continued social acceptance. Accordingly, we concede to our jobs an outsized portion of our self-identity.

While the promise of a paycheck offers a veneer of stability, future uncertainty renders the veneer only marginally comforting. People speak of "job security" without appreciating the oxymoronic nature of the phrase. A job offers security insofar as the employee can trade hours for dollars. Remove that ability— through health crisis, economic disruption, corporate restructuring, outsourcing, natural disaster, etc.—and the security turns ephemeral.

Unemployment wounds most deeply those who cling to job-based identities. The saga of unemployment that followed the 2008-09 financial crisis, when white-collar professionals went from earning six-figures to scratching for entry-level jobs at Wal-Mart, exemplifies the fragility of identities dependent on occupational status. The mental anguish associated with loss of occupational identity represents one aspect of fragility. The budgetary anguish associated with loss of purchasing power comprises a more visceral aspect, defining fragility in increments of worry that grow as disposable income shrinks—the smaller the safety margin, the greater the worry.

As a child witnessing my father's bout with unemployment in the 1980s, sensing the psychological and emotional angst that gripped the household, I perhaps developed a subconscious predisposition to savings. At age fifteen, working my first after-school job at a supermarket, I saw savings as a beacon that offered hope in a stressful den of shouting bosses and pushy customers. Midway through college, squirreling away the proceeds from various odd jobs, I attained a $20,000 nest egg (the equivalent of $37,000 in 2018), which, at my father's recommendation, I deployed in mutual funds just as the bull market of the 1990's gained steam. By the time I started my post-college career, I routinely banked half my take home pay. A decade later, in my late thirties, I attained enough in savings and investments to initiate a meaningful income-investing program. The proceeds covered my basic expenses. At that point, I routinely invested the entire take-home pay from my job. As I write this, on the doorstep of early retirement, I save and invest an annualized sum greater than my entire gross pay as a newly salaried communications director.

Those with a penchant for instant gratification may find this Horatio Alger narrative of little inspirational value. The savings mentality necessary to habitually squirrel away fifty percent or more of one's disposable income represents a form of Puritan austerity so contrary to the mainstream as to render it a curiosity.

People who adopt such a mentality in youth, when the siren song of material pleasure readily depletes the pocketbook, expose themselves to the sneers of consumer culture, which labels them derisively as "misers" and "tightwads." The tendency of an extreme savings regimen to generate criticism rather than applause reveals much about the sad state of mainstream money maturity. A culture that increasingly embraces lotteries, casinos, and penny stock promotions as "wealth building" schemes will find little appeal in a savings protocol that comes to fruition only after years of hard work and deprivation. Yet while lotteries, casinos, and penny-stock promotions rarely lead to fortunes*, a savings protocol reliably provides the seed from which future fortune sprouts. No honest examination of financial awareness can proceed without recognizing the primacy of savings. Achieving the transition from spender to saver marks the first milestone of money maturity and provides a launchpad to the attainment of further milestones.

The Stages of Money Maturity

Cash Craft philosophy regards money as a skill, a process by which one progresses through stages of awareness, delineated as follows:

◆Early Stage (a.k.a. "Apprentice"), dominated by the struggle to achieve a savings mentality and the attributes conducive to sustainable high savings rates

◆Middle Stage (a.k.a. "Craftsman"), dominated by the development of an investing mindset and the attributes conducive to risk awareness

◆Advanced Stage (a.k.a. "Master"), dominated by the development of a dividend snowball that allows the investor to transition from financial freedom to financial abundance.

---

* The authors of *The Millionaire Next Door* estimate the chance of the average adult gaining windfall wealth at less than one in four thousand.

Money Milestone	Key Investor Trait
Savings Mentality	Recognizes cash as an asset
High Savings Rate	Efficiently transforms labor into capital
Risk Awareness	Deploys capital to productive use
Investor Mindset	Avoids liabilities that masquerade as valuable things
Dividend Snowball	Manages portfolio as a business enterprise
Financial Abundance	Generates six-figure annual passive income

Significant milestones of Cash Craft philosophy and the behavioral traits necessary to achieve them

The early stage describes financial awareness in its most basic form, and encompasses a timeline in which money apprentices face several initial struggles: economically, their security depends on others; psychologically, they feel the attraction of binge spending and instant gratification; socially, they face the pressure of a consumer culture that promotes debt as a passport to unsustainable lifestyles. Against these struggles, a savings mentality offers insulation. Lacking it, the money apprentice remains mired in the unpleasantry which capitalism inflicts on those who lack capital.

Perceiving Cash as an Asset

Money apprentices face a financial relationship in which money, at least initially, enjoys a predominance of power. The apprentice, asset-poor, suffers a disadvantage: to gain the pleasure of money's company, something rather mundane, he or she must sacrifice a precious, irreplaceable resource—time. Transposed into the realm of human relations this dynamic reveals its cruelty. Imagine a scenario in which the object of attraction demands, as a prerequisite for a date, the sacrifice of a favorite pet, the destruction of childhood photos, or the permanent loss of some other cherished item. Given such conditions, people of reasonable self-esteem might express shock and an appropriate expletive. Yet when money demands of its suitor the sacrifice of life's irreplaceable hours, people accept it as standard procedure. Recognizing this absurd dynamic qualifies as a key lesson in the development of a savings mentality.

When trading hours for dollars represents the dominant financial paradigm, the money apprentice has only one way to place money on more equal terms: increase the quantity of money per unit of time. Here, the power of savings plays a subtle but increasingly significant role. So little appreciation remains for the thrift mindset of past generations that many people dismiss as a trite platitude Ben Franklin's famous observation, "a penny saved is a penny earned." Though three centuries of monetary mayhem require an inflation-adjusted update of the aphorism, they don't negate the key idea: savings impart to earnings a multiplier effect.

In the money game, a paycheck alone means nothing, unless one sets aside a portion—retained earnings, in balance sheet terminology—that represents a transformation of labor into capital. The power of savings goes beyond its balance sheet boost. Due to the time value of money, a phenomenon by which uncertainty renders present dollars more valuable than future dollars, saving hedges inflation risk. It also hedges the income stagnation that, adjusted for inflation, attributes to the average paycheck the same purchasing power today as forty years ago. Effectively, it functions as an insurance policy, its premium paid by a simple act of short-term forbearance.

My investment club mentors once gave me an interesting perspective on savings psychology. When I mentioned a news report that lamented how half of Americans lacked the cash to cover a five-hundred dollar emergency[*], Bill, a club elder,

---

[*] Aimee Picchi, "Most Americans Can't Handle a $500 Surprise Bill," CBS News, Jan. 6, 2016

responded by digging from his wallet a stack of currency and telling me to run my fingers along the surface of the notes.

"Do you know what this is?" he asked.

"Cash," I replied, feeling the edges of the greenbacks.

"No," he said. "Look past the façade. Really, it's a *choice*—a choice between present consumption or future investment. Some consider it a symbol of potential. Each dollar in this stack represents a potential worker that, employed in the enterprise of my investment portfolio, will tirelessly produce a stream of income. If I spend them, I lose forever their productive potential. Understand? An investor looks at a dollar bill and sees its productive potential. As you probably realize, most Americans aren't investors."

Initially, I considered this lesson an indulgence in wordplay, and doubted if referring to currency as a "choice" altered its intrinsic nature. However, the more I understood club philosophy, the more I recognized its guidance not only for portfolio strategy but for life. Words matter, because they have the power to influence thoughts. In turn, thoughts matter, because they have the power to influence reality. Referring to the cash in his wallet as "productive potential" helped Bill's foreground the financial aspect of his life. Though well-off beyond the means of most Americans, he refused to take his financial freedom for granted.

Since the personal finance genre already boasts numerous titles with savings-oriented advice, I won't pursue a lengthy examination of the psychological and social habits that contribute to savings, other than to remark upon a basic truth: big numbers grow from small numbers, a process on which time and commitment exert great effect. Vincent Van Gogh once famously observed that "great things are not done by impulse, but by a series of small things brought together." As with art, so with personal finance: patient savers make patient investors, and patience counts as a key attribute for successful income investing.

A friend once confided proudly that after years of struggling with debt, she had managed to save ten thousand dollars. Now that she had some money, she wanted to "get in the game." What investing ideas, she wondered, did I recommend? Impatient by nature, she found my advice disappointing. Don't get in the game, I told her, without a better understanding of its rules. Though a decent improvement over old habits, her 10K barely met the minimum standard of an emergency fund, as defined by the traditional metric of six months' expenses. Keep the cash in the bank, I suggested; when she saved her next ten thousand, I might recommend a more productive use.

Cash ranks as an asset, its merit measured more by security than productivity, and gaining enough for short-term protection against job loss or sudden expense counts as an important success in the cultivation of savings mentality. Additional success comes through increased savings rate and consistency. Again, referencing *minimum* standards, saving 10% from regular income sources measures progress for the money apprentice, while saving 20% to 30% merits applause. Eventually, to achieve real money momentum, the apprentice will need a savings rate of 50% or higher. Since the average American saves from 3% to 5% of disposable income, these savings rate goals may entail considerable lifestyle alteration. However, tolerating a single-digit savings rate delays the higher money milestones so far into the future that they lose their inspirational allure. At a savings rate of 5%, the first 100K net worth milestone, described by investing guru Charlie Munger as the hardest net worth hurdle, requires the saver to earn over a span of several years the cumulative equivalent of about two million dollars in post-tax income. Since the low-paying jobs typical of the early stage apprentice make such cumulative earnings unlikely in a reasonable time frame, a high savings rate, coupled with a decent cash stash, gives some power to people otherwise disadvantaged in the money game.

Echoes of Charlie Munger and the importance of the 100K net worth hurdle resonated in a conversation I once had with Bill. Sympathetic to the plight of recent college grads, many of whom face the double burden of student loan debt and entry-level work in cities with high costs of living, I wondered what perspective a seasoned income investor might offer a demographic barely able to save a few hundred dollars per month. When I remarked that today's economic realities confront young adults with hardships that make an income portfolio seem like a pipe dream, Bill adopted the tone of a soapbox orator:

"What perspective would I give a broke college grad? Guess what—I was a broke college grad. . .I know the details of that life, and I'd give this perspective, without sugar-coating the truth. I'd say you need an emergency fund, 10K minimum, and you need it ASAP, by whatever legal means available— a second job, mowing lawns, collecting scrap metal, whatever. Then you need to set that money aside in a way that keeps it mentally inaccessible, perhaps in a series of laddered short-term CDs. It's a small step, but absolutely crucial, to the extent that maintaining an emergency fund provides a test of money management potential. It may sound callous, but people unable to amass an emergency fund, or who amass the fund but repeatedly raid the money for non-emergency use, face life management issues that make them poor stewards of a bank account, let alone an investment portfolio. . .

"With an emergency fund set aside, you should focus all your energies on attaining 100K in liquid net worth. I don't mean net worth by the traditional metric of assets minus liabilities; I mean 100K in liquid investable funds. This will require major sacrifice, because the bulk of it will result from savings alone, but as such it signifies your ability to perceive cash as an asset and make positive wealth choices. I'd say you need that 100K by your early thirties, roughly by age thirty-two or thirty-three, though obtaining it may well entail unpleasant lifestyle constraints that invite mockery by less-thrifty friends. In practice it probably means saving an average of a thousand dollars a month between graduation and your early thirties. If you can save more, great—but you can't save much less."

Here Bill paused for effect and warned that his next ideas might challenge unconventional financial advice:

"At some point on the path to 100K, probably around 50K, you'll need to open a brokerage account and begin putting money into plain vanilla mutual funds. I'll suggest an unorthodox approach: don't reinvest dividends, and don't invest for growth. Even now, at this early stage, the emphasis should be on nurturing cash flow. Have dividends swept to cash and then invest that cash at year's end. Yes, I know financial planners recommend young investors to concentrate on equity growth during the accumulation phase of a portfolio. But accumulation phase protocols don't apply to income portfolios. Accumulation phase implies drawdown phase, and income portfolios, properly constructed, don't suffer drawdown phase depletion. It's best to regard the income portfolio as a pool of permanent capital. Once capital goes in, it doesn't come out...

"As I stated, the emphasis even at this point should be on nurturing cash flow. It won't be much, because we don't yet want to venture very far out on the risk spectrum. Rather, we need to safeguard our hard-won capital. Regarding investment choices, this means emphasizing quality over productivity. Specifically, it means a Ginnie Mae bond fund. I'd use Vanguard's VFIIX. But with a portfolio of 50K, you can dabble in some higher yield investment grade stuff too. I'd put 20K in cash, 10K in VFIIX, 10K in PONAX (the PIMCO Income Fund, the largest actively managed bond fund on the planet), and 5K each in IVOL and BKT. Note: this does not include your emergency fund. That's completely separate. Altogether, this allocation should net you about $100 per month in dividends—not much, but we're progressing incrementally into the productivity zone. Over the course of the year, this equates to $1,200, just over what you are supposed to contribute each month in savings. And that's how you should think of your portfolio's productivity at this point—as a month of free savings."

Noting the mainstream financial premise that cash and bond funds serve better as anchors for retirement nest eggs than as core holdings for young professionals, I wondered if attaining 100K in liquid net worth by age thirty-two or thirty-three required more aggressive investments.

"No, not at this point," Bill replied. "With less than 100K in net worth, you still remain in what we might call the apprentice stage of money maturity. Even if you have a great interest in learning about the investing world and cultivating a more sophisticated awareness of risk, your life priorities should center on apprentice stage milestones: career, salary, and savings. At this point, net worth gains accrue more reliably from savings than from market dynamics. Let's say you put the entirety of your 50K brokerage balance into stocks. Suppose further that the market delivered a ten percent gain for that year. Hey, you've made 5K! Obviously, that's better than the $1,200 you'd get per my recommendation. But let's put that 5K in perspective. You staked your entire portfolio to get it, and still only achieved the equivalent of five months of savings. Since you could gain one month of savings equivalent for much less risk, you have to ask if the four additional months of savings gains adequately compensated for the jeopardy to capital."

Bill went on to answer the question by ascribing a two-fold purpose to his unusually conservative portfolio suggestion. First, because investment losses inflict disproportionate pain on people struggling through the Five Figure Swamp—eroding assets that took greater sacrifice than for wealthier investors, the money apprentice must exercise extreme caution when venturing into the productivity zone: *"To realistically attain a million-dollar portfolio in your forties, you need 100K in liquid assets by your early thirties. For most college grads, this implies surpassing the 100K hurdle within seven or eight years of graduation. Boosting salary and savings rates will achieve this much more reliably and with less jeopardy to capital than market dynamics, though it may mean enduring an unpleasant combination of ramen and roommates longer than you'd like."*

The second reason for Bill's conservativism had to do with the way income investors perceive the role of equities in an income portfolio: *"If the goal is reliable monthly cash flow, then the aspiring rentier should prioritize quality over excitement. True income investors own equities for one reason—the organic income growth that results from dividend increases. Accordingly, capital gains represent a distraction, and the money apprentice shouldn't prioritize them. A ten percent dividend boost matters more for long-term productivity than a ten percent capital gain. That's the proper way to regard productive potential."*

Perceiving cash as an asset turns more intuitive when, with time, the nest egg grows and begins to throw off interest—a taste of the passive income that the wise apprentice will crave to increase. Though still on the treadmill, trading hours for dollars, the apprentice senses a nascent calculus pointing the way to escape from the rat race. Though a full explication of savings mentality could require a book unto itself, the following traits greatly assist the process:

--a willingness to associate with a peer-group whose values reinforce financial success

To dramatize how spendthrift habits can threaten wealth building, members of the investment club often recollected stories of acquaintances who, as young adults, preferred indulgence to investment. Mostly, these anecdotes provided cautionary tales of characters for whom the initial thrill of money making only subsidized behavioral shortcomings. Flush with cash after a stint on an oil rig, or a construction project, or a season on a fishing boat, these youths easily succumbed to episodes of wild spending that often left them with nothing but memories to show for their labors. Clifton, a club member famous for pithy remarks that summarized investment club conversations, punctuated these stories with the observation that "youth and fat wallets make a reckless combination." Since the innate passions of youth tend to center on the pursuit of pleasure, even strong-willed apprentice wealth builders prove vulnerable to binge spending, particularly if their peer-group revels in such behavior. To the extent that positive peer values insulate apprentice wealth builders from innate negative tendencies, the investment club sought to model and inspire such positivity.

--a professional ethic that facilitates the transition from low income to high income

Cash Craft philosophy defines a "high" income as one in the top 10% of wage earners. The basis for this definition has more to do with practical logistics than income-bracket braggadocio. Only with a top 10% income (by 2018 standards, roughly 100K+) can the money apprentice realize the high savings rates—fifty percent or better—necessary to gain equal terms with money in a reasonable time frame. In addition to funding a supercharged savings regimen, a high income confers a psychological benefit, making more palatable the risk-management mindset necessary for investment success and progress through the higher stages of financial awareness.

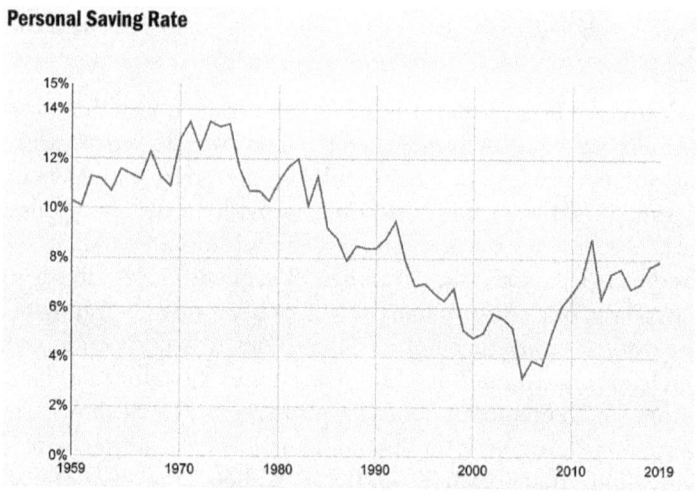

Average personal savings rate of U.S households, 1959-2020. (Source: St. Louis Fed/Brookings Inst.)

By personal experience, I know savers with moderate or low incomes can achieve high savings rates. However, to do so over the long term requires such sacrifice or reduced living standards as to render it unsustainable for most people. By linking high savings with high income, the investment club signaled its recognition that modern costs of living present obstacles to early stage money apprentices. When those costs include the burden of taxes, the struggle faced by those trying to build wealth via earned income turns more frustrating. Even the glitter of six-figure pay loses its shine when subjected to the erosion of deductions and taxes. However, if a dream of early retirement provides the primary motive for income investing proficiency, then one must face a daunting reality: to retire early with an investment portfolio capable of funding a "fatFIRE" lifestyle (100K+ annual passive income), investors must save, in their late thirties and through their forties, annual sums in the 50K to 70K range. (The savings burden proves a bit less heavy for those with defined-benefit pensions, an increasingly rare perquisite of career life.)

Money Milestone Synergy

Readers cynical about the prospect of saving each year what the average American household spends should consider that I eventually managed just such a savings regimen in my own path to wealth, and I claim nothing particularly remarkable in my resume. Rather, what I demonstrated—adherence to a philosophy and dedication to a plan—most people can implement. True, we each face unique obstacles, some more insurmountable than others. My investment club mentors didn't promise success to all who study their principles. Rather, they claimed that lessons associated with the money milestones make progression to higher level financial success more likely. The club presented the stages of money-maturity not as a prescriptive how-to manual, but as part of a descriptive income investing philosophy that, with varying outcomes, people could apply to beneficial effect.

Though I didn't know it at the time, my own money-apprentice years developed in a manner generally reflective of investment club philosophy. Dislike of my first job gave me a savings mindset, which helped me turn the unpleasant exchange of hours for dollars into a more empowering transformation of labor into capital. As a college student who pursued an advanced degree en-route to a managerial position in communications, I transformed the character of my work from job-oriented shift completion to career-oriented creativity, a process that gave me the benefits of a stable profession, community connection, and upstanding peer-group values. Finally, the effort to advance my career resulted in progressively higher income, eventually in the six-figure realm, bolstering both my savings rate and my resolve to deploy increasingly greater sums into investments. The synergy of these milestones, combined with investment returns, helped grow the 100K nest egg that I possessed at age thirty-two into a 500K portfolio by the time I reached forty. At that point, dividends and interest from my portfolio covered my living expenses, allowing me to save and invest my entire after-tax salary (roughly 50K, and then reaching 70K annually)—and, again boosted by market returns, double my portfolio to one million by the time I turned forty-seven. Though these numbers reflect attributes beyond the typical money apprentice, I can state with confidence that any higher-level milestones I accrued grew from the rootstock of lower-level achievements—achievements, in turn, built on a foundation of patience and perseverance. Put another way, I owe my millionaire status in no small measure to life lessons learned as a teenager working a "nickel and dime" job.

Apprentice Stage Hazards

While my story provides an example of what can go right when money milestones align, valuable lessons await in anecdotes about the pitfalls, accidents, and behavioral choices that, for many people, make cultivation of a savings mentality less than assured. Frequently, money apprentices fall short of their promise by prematurely facing higher-level choices—in other words, responsibilities better saved for advanced-stage maturity. Marriage and pregnancy may create the burden of parenthood, with its emotional and mental demands, at precisely the time the saver should focus on career development. A big purchase, requiring debt and its legacy of interest payments, may deprive a savings regimen of momentum. Sometimes, people fall short because they achieve one milestone but neglect the others. For example, a person may transition from job to career, yet remain a spender, as happens frequently among those who pursue high-status professions that encourage displays of conspicuous consumption.

The most egregious money mishaps of the apprentice stage occur when people temporarily achieve high income without gaining a savings mentality. The mishaps that result frequently lead to the squandering of potential good fortune. I remember well a conversation the investment club had about an unemployed couple who went from living on charity and State assistance to a $670,000 windfall from the lottery. "Blessed" with what they perceived as sudden riches, the couple proceeded to buy two brand-new SUVs, a fixer-upper house, gift a substantial sum to their church, and launch a business venture. After subjecting the couple's decisions to scrutiny—lamenting the destruction of capital represented in buying brand-new cars, the burden of liabilities represented in a fixer-upper house, and the foolishness of a business venture statistically likely to fail—the investment club gurus pondered the couple's future. Bill, interjecting after a moment of aloof thoughtfulness, observed that a cruel irony characterizes human behavior and the management of wealth. Those who most need windfall cash, and dream of lottery winnings or inheritance, prove least capable of wisely handling it. "*Lacking experience with income- producing capital, emotional spenders can't appreciate the sacrifice and patience involved in the acquisition of wealth, and consequently deplete windfall cash in a short time,*" Bill asserted. "*Those who need a windfall least—the nurturers already in possession of wealth—prove most capable of handling a windfall wisely.*"

This comment leads me to reflect, in closing, on a subtle but important aspect of money maturity, an aspect hinted at in Bill's idea about cash representing a choice between present consumption or future investment. At its essence, the cultivation of savings encompasses a mental and emotional struggle over the perception of money. Those who channel the correct perception, retaining money for productive use, gain resources necessary for advancement to higher levels of financial awareness. Those who channel the wrong perception, squandering money in unproductive consumption, suffer the unpleasantry which capitalism inflicts upon those who lack capital.

Afterword:
Income Investing as a Philosophical Approach to Money

> *The following conversation, set amid the outdoor dining patio of Gladstone's (an iconic seafood restaurant at the intersection of Sunset Blvd. and PCH), presents the highlights of a lunchtime interview that took place between the author and manuscript editor in the early summer of 2020. Soft breezes and the antics of seagulls prod a lighthearted mood, a welcome respite from the disquietude of pandemic-fueled headlines.*

R. Beachley: Care for a beer? I recommend Peroni or Blue Moon.

Editor: *Why Peroni or Blue Moon?*

R. Beachley: Altria owns a 10% stake in InBev, and as an Altria shareholder, I get dividends resulting from sales of InBev brands.

Editor: *So, in the midst of perhaps the worst pandemic in a century, you manage to obsess over dividends?*

R. Beachley: Of course! But we're not here to discuss the politics of capitalism, right? You mentioned you have some questions about the book manuscript.

Editor: *Yes, and about income investing more generally. First, let me express my appreciation for involving me in the project. The meditations opened the door to a financial perspective—really, a philosophy of money—which I never before considered. However, I anticipate that many readers might say the book holds both allure and vexation. It's like you've taken us to an amazing vista point, dissembled the view into a jigsaw puzzle, and left us pondering how the pieces fit together.*

R. Beachley: Sorry, but I can't think of a more fitting description of the investing world than "alluring and vexing," so perhaps it's only appropriate that those words describe a book on the subject. Frankly a bit of vexation might do people some good. Those who persevere may find it opens the door to a more useful perspective. People reflexively want answers, when maybe they should prefer questions. Also, I didn't set out to write a "how-to" manual.

Editor: *My background as an English professor puts me in the habit of looking for themes. I find myself searching for a guiding principle, a unifying idea that I can wrap like a ribbon around the meditations. Instead I find a set of motifs: the emphasis on cash flow over capital gain, the stability of income relative to price, the hazards of "leanFIRE," the perception of cash as an asset, etc. What do you think comprises the book's main idea, that readers might consider the key takeaway?*

R. Beachley: I think maybe English professors need to get over their need for unifying ideas. It only perpetuates a fixation on simple answers! But I'll play along. I think maybe you really want to ask a different question: what concept guides the theory and practice of income investing? Unfortunately, the answer might only lead to complications.

Editor: *I guess if it didn't, then you wouldn't have material for a book, right? So, what's the answer?*

R. Beachley: In basic terms, income investors make assets the means by which they afford indulgence. Put another way, income investors limit their spending to the cash flows their assets provide.

Editor: *Seems fairly straightforward. What's the complication?*

R. Beachley: Mostly the definition of terms. How do we define "asset?" Income investors apply a ruthlessly simple requirement to the term: assets produce cash flow. Mainstream finance allows a more lenient perspective, and applies the term even to things like gold, cryptocurrency, and start-up companies that don't produce cash flow.

Editor: *It seems the emphasis on this definition makes income investors a unique subset of the investing population.*

R. Beachley: It makes them a unique subset of the human population. In financial terms, you can divide the world in two categories: things that take cash away, and things that put cash in your pocket. If something depletes cash, we call it a liability. If something produces cash, we call it an asset. Income investors collect assets. The majority of people collect liabilities.

Editor: *I wonder if perhaps this makes finance arbitrarily dualistic. Couldn't there be a third category, where something—say, a rental property—costs money, but also produces cash flow? Or what about jewelry and fine art—they don't produce cash flow, but still count in the value of an estate.*

R. Beachley: Well, you call attention to a primary hazard of liabilities. They often masquerade as valuable things! Perceiving the liability in something that appears valuable requires great discipline. But since you've mentioned some specific items, we can subject them to a bit of scrutiny to see if they merit our hard-won capital. The rental property MIGHT qualify as an asset, if, immediately upon purchase, the present value of the benefits (e.g. the rental income) exceeds the present value of the costs. But we'd need to consider other factors too. Does it truly offer passive income, or does it force me to screen tenants and fix late night plumbing problems? Remember, I want an asset, not a job. Additionally, I need to measure it according to the quality/productivity rubric. Perhaps the rental income arrives sporadically or potentially suffers disruption due to fire or flood, rendering its quality suspect. If I want to play in the real estate space, and I can get a 7% yield from the preferred stock of a mortgage REIT like Annaly Capital, a security with a long history of steady dividend payments, or if I can get 8%-10% yields from mortgage/asset backed bond closed-end funds run by skilled managers like PIMCO, why do I want to mess around with the rental property? It would have to offer something really compelling, like 15% yield on cost. The point—cash flow potential isn't enough. An asset produces cash flows that rank highly on the quality/productivity rubric.

Editor: *Where do things like careers fit in? In your meditation on financial abundance, you argue that careers don't count as assets, yet financial advisors consistently remind us that our ability to earn counts as one of our greatest resources. Don't careers put money in our pockets, and thus belong in the asset category?*

R. Beachley: A career puts money in your pocket, but only in exchange for time, an irreplaceable resource. Your accountant, conforming to traditional balance sheet metrics, would not regard it as a liability, but in our life ledger we have to perceive it as such. The world abounds in money, but our lives don't abound in time. It's not even close to an equitable exchange. Also, not to nitpick, but people don't really "own" a career. Insofar as you remain of sound body and mind, you have an ability to exchange hours for dollars. You might find the exchange beneficial and satisfying, but it costs the most precious resource you have.

Editor: *That's depressing! Maybe I should abandon this line of inquiry before I learn more unpleasant news. But since I asked, what about jewelry and fine art?*

R. Beachley: Again, we can apply the quality/productivity rubric. Perhaps jewelry and fine art possess "quality" of a sort—and if so, I'd want them insured, an immediate and recurring cost—but they offer little productivity, unless I put them on display and charge people to see them. No, most people who collect jewelry and art—if they have an interest in the financial component—care about price appreciation. And maybe, if I really knew the collectibles market, I could get a profitable result. But, in the attempt, I'd be engaging in speculation. I prefer investing to speculation.

Editor: *So, just to clarify: if something requires price appreciation to produce a profitable result, it doesn't qualify as an asset?*

R. Beachley: It doesn't even qualify as an investment. If your strategy requires you to buy something for "X" and sell for "X + 5," or some other number that reflects greater fools bidding up prices, you engage in speculation, not investing. A true investment doesn't need to produce a capital gain to rank well on the quality/productivity rubric. It might produce a capital gain, but the investor doesn't require it. Again, consider preferred stock, a security class from which I have obtained significant profitable result, buying at par and redeeming at par, without ever realizing a capital gain. The money came entirely from dividends.

Editor: *Why do you suppose the income approach, and the willingness to disregard capital gain, doesn't get more traction among market participants and the financial media?*

R. Beachley: Probably the biggest reason is practical, but let's consider first the psychological reasons. Dividends make boring headlines. When was the last time you turned on the financial news and heard excited voices listing that day's dividend declarations? Additionally, the average person sees the stock market in terms of price action. "Did the market go up or down today?" Rarely do people regard stocks for what they really represent—an ownership stake in a company, conferring a right to share in the company's cash flows. Ultimately, though, the practical consideration deters many. Income may be more stable than price, but only a substantial portfolio, 400K-500K minimum, produces sustainable income at a meaningful level.

Editor: *I get the sense, based on certain passages in your book, that you consider such a portfolio more achievable than people realize. To invoke a memorable phrase, you say "wealth simply represents cash flow subjected to the catalyst of time and good money habits." Applying the catalyst doesn't require any special magic, right?*

R. Beachley: Maybe not magic, but it does require special commitment. Wealth builders who achieve the money milestones outlined in Cash Craft philosophy position themselves for a notable end goal: an earlier-than-average retirement funded by a greater-than-average income. Knowing the power of specificity, my investment club colleagues interpreted this to mean a *rentier* lifestyle funded by a passive income of 100K or greater. Global wealth statistics rank this as exceptional*. People have to want it, the way a mountain climber hungers for a summit, and the sacrifice involved may well prod the classic question of mountaineering:

---

* An April 15, 2019 Washington Post article by Michelle Singletary reported that just 1% of U.S. investors still in the workforce could save the 50% of income necessary to build a robust early retirement nest egg. According to the 2018 Retirement Confidence Survey from the Employee Benefit Research Institute, only 3% of workers expect to retire before 55, and 15% *by* 55.

why bother? I raise the question because people often regard the completion of apprentice stage milestones—savings, career, and high income—sufficient for a decent lifestyle. When career and income provide satisfaction, the incentive necessary to progress through the higher stages of money maturity may diminish, especially if the aspiring *rentier* sees acquaintances crash and burn in investment schemes gone awry. If trading hours for dollars feels like an enjoyable exercise, and contemplating life after work brings only thoughts of loneliness and boredom, then the prospect of time freedom may lose its allure. On the other hand, if the prospect of a *rentier* lifestyle during the robust years of middle age inspires the imagination, then time freedom provides the doorway to dreams. But you have to WANT it. You have to identify a retirement vision that provides sufficient motivation. And you have to determine what sacrifices you'll make to achieve it.

Editor: *So, ultimately, income investing represents a desire for time freedom.*

R. Beachley: Either implicitly or explicitly, yes. It's not about the income *per se*, but rather the unshackled life that the sustainability of that income makes possible.

Editor: *You write that the universe doesn't really care how much money we have or which social functions we attend, but rather that we live interesting, adventurous lives. Can you comment on this? What blueprint guides an unshackled life?*

R. Beachley: Admittedly, I'm still trying to figure that one out! At the very least, it means we have a willingness to jettison our workplace identities and the psychological dynamics—the power games—that workplace identities encourage. Going further, I think it means we try to get past the accumulation mindset that our culture finds so seductive. It's not easy to do this, especially if you've paid dues on the hours-for-dollars treadmill and developed a taste for the material rewards it supplies. But I don't think we can discover our true selves unless we relinquish these mindsets.

Editor: *I can imagine here a chorus of dissent from the ranks of career professionals. Suppose someone finds the treadmill enjoyable. Why jettison an enjoyable occupational identify?*

R. Beachley: Ironically, people who enjoy their jobs make the best candidates for early retirement, because they approach the non-occupational life from a position of strength rather than frustration. I suspect, however, that if we subject the treadmill achievers to the true test of enjoyment—a willingness to work for free—we'd find their enthusiasm for the workplace considerably diminished. Let's use you as an example. I've known you since grad school, and you've told me more than once that you've never had a bad day in your teaching career. But let me ask you this: would you grade papers for free?

Editor: *Not a chance!*

R. Beachley: Now that I've got you in the hot seat, let's explore the matter a bit further, and contrast the professional use of your writing ability, as applied to your teaching career, with its creative use, as applied to your literary pursuits. You recently published a travel memoir, right? Think about the hundreds of hours you devoted to that book! Having some familiarity with the publishing world, you knew from the outset that the effort was very unlikely to result in much financial gain. We might say, in fact, that you undertook the work for free. Yet you did so gladly. Why?

Editor: *When weeks go by without a sale, I really wonder. I guess you have some thoughts?*

R. Beachley: I think so. I think deep down you sense that grading another stack of papers won't bring much joy to the world, while books like your travel memoir, with its unique glimpse of life on a remote Pacific island, at least have the potential to do so. It's a simple premise: we bring joy to the world by creating things we and others enjoy. And how do we know we enjoy something? Because we do it for free.

Editor: *Wow. . .I guess that really puts our life priorities into perspective. But don't some people get paid to do what they love?*

R. Beachley: Well sure. . .and perhaps in an ideal economy, passion would determine occupation for everyone. Imagine if only those who love cooking staffed our fast food kitchens. A visit to

McDonald's would mean a rich culinary experience! But we don't have an ideal economy. Most people work at jobs that stifle their passions.

Editor: *With that in mind, why do you take a cynical view of "leanFIRE?" I mean, suppose someone has a decent portfolio—for example, Marlon's F-U money, which you referenced in your meditation on financial abundance. If the pursuit of passion means living in my RV and going off the grid, why not quit the cubicle?*

R. Beachley: Well, I admit my meditations, at times, take on the tone of a jaded sell-out who traded youthful dreams for comfort and a pension. But let me offer this perspective. The fans of leanFIRE should realize that I too once harbored a leanFIRE obsession. Head full of sailboat dreams, I quested, in my thirties, for a lifestyle built on a budget of $2,500 per month, and by age thirty-eight had a portfolio to implement it with investment income alone. Yet resources couldn't quell doubt. Hesitation to quit my job, research into the true costs of sailing, and the ridicule of my investment club mentors caused me to delay and eventually reconsider. "You have almost 500K in net worth," my mentors admonished. "You're on the verge of some real money momentum!" Look, it's not like I take a cynical view of leanFIRE *per se*, but rather the excessive praise that the concept generates in personal finance media. The bloggers and writers who sing the praises of the work-optional life highlight the benefits but rarely discuss the drawbacks. By drawback, I mean the opportunity cost of a path that sacrifices a chance at money momentum for more immediate pleasures. And let's be honest: living in a RV to indulge an off-the-grid lifestyle might offer fulfillment in your thirties, but the allure changes as you get older, when your pursuits take on more sophisticated and refined forms. And imagine your older self, trapped in the RV, chained to an increasingly unfulfilling path, which you can't escape because you sacrificed money momentum for a leanFIRE life.

Editor: *But must I really hold on for "fatFIRE?" What's so special about 100K in passive income?*

R. Beachley: There's nothing particularly special about it, other than the audacious rarity it merits in the statistics of global wealth. However, it's not completely arbitrary. It aligns closely with the "happiness threshold" identified in several surveys and sociological studies. The studies show that while making less than 100K, and especially less than 75K, correlates more with unhappiness, making more than 100K does not produce meaningful happiness improvement. So, the 100K range seems to represent a happiness/budget sweet spot. I readily admit, however, that it might prove inadequate for certain spendthrift personalities. Probably these personalities wouldn't succeed as income investors anyway. But keep in mind, no less a penthouse-dweller than Warren Buffet has endorsed the 100K happiness threshold.*

Editor: *So, maybe it's not an arbitrary number. . .but is it an enduring number? Maybe I should ask the question this way: Cash Craft philosophy aims for a fairly lofty budget and net worth realm, for which leanFIRE and even the million-dollar portfolio comprise mere stepping-stones. You state it requires about 1.5 to 2 million dollars. How do you think people might regard these numbers in ten or twenty years?*

R. Beachley: Maybe come back and ask me in ten or twenty years! Look, here's the paradox: the perfect retirement plan doesn't exist. If you wait for one to materialize, the lifestyle vision that motivated your initial planning might dissipate. Lifestyle inflation, and the number-creep that results from it, probably keeps more people on the treadmill than market events or economic concerns. The 100K budget, and the requisite 1.5 to 2 million in cash-generating assets, offers (in my view) a reasonable intersection of fulfillment and sustainability. For most people—perhaps not princes or jet-setting celebrities, but most people—it satisfies not only needs but a good deal of wants. Moreover, I contend that if you can't design an interesting and enjoyable retirement around a 100K annual budget, the net income equivalent of a 150K gross

---

* Clifford, Catharine. "Warren Buffet Is Worth 75 Billion but Says He Would Be "Very Happy with 100,000 a Year." CNBC, July 12, 2017.

salary, then you probably have psychological and emotional issues that no financial metric will allay. Additionally, I present the "cash craft" metrics as a counterpoint to the glittering generalities prevalent in personal finance literature. People looking for "wealth secrets" find an easy seduction in books and blogs that promote gimmicky ideas and clever phrases. These phrases sound compelling but offer no objective guidepost to help readers assess progress. As in the business world, success in the arena of personal finance requires people to identify specific goals and timeframes. You can't just say "I want to make a lot of money" or "I want to retire early." You need specificity, like "I want to increase my income by ten percent this year" or "I want 3K per month in passive income by 40." Specificity catalyzes progress. The cash craft goal of 100K offers a clear guidepost. The goal might prove too lofty, but at least it offers a metric for progress.

Editor: *Do you regard all personal finance literature cynically?*

R. Beachley: Not all of it. There are some excellent titles that belong on the bookshelf of anyone serious about investing. But maybe that's the distinction—the better titles focus more on investing than personal finance and provide philosophical inquiry more than how-to guidance. Benjamin Graham's *The Intelligent Investor* has to rank near the top. I also value Anette Thau's *The Bond Book* for its thorough overview of bond market dynamics. George Clason's *The Richest Man in Babylon* offers an entertaining yet informative perspective, told in parable form, on the acquisition of wealth. I took care in my meditations to reference other relevant titles. However, when books sell readers on gimmicky ideas, I view them much more cynically. Tim Ferris has probably gained more success selling the idea of the four-hour workweek than anybody has achieved implementing it. Publishers see a lucrative marketing potential in such gimmicks, because they inject a dose of hope into the frustrated finances of the masses. People familiar with the statistics of global wealth know the faulty basis for such "hopium." Less than 1% of the population controls assets of one million dollars or greater. We should expect a higher percentage if the self-help books actually produced what they promote.

Editor: *Are income investors always so depressing? From our conversation, I've learned careers don't count as an asset, and self-help books don't really help. How should the aspiring "rentier" proceed to get off the treadmill in a reasonable timeframe?*

R. Beachley: By implementing the tried and true steps utilized since ancient times. Cherish savings and deploy it to productive use. Collect assets and limit liabilities. Cultivate risk awareness and invest accordingly. Develop a sufficiently inspirational retirement vision to help guide the quest. But I'll add this bit of personal commentary as supplement. The aspiring rentier might find comfort and confidence in my example. I'm nothing special. I worked the same nickel-and-dime jobs as other teenagers and young adults. I never had the clout of a prestigious degree or special connections. True, I derived a boost from a defined benefit pension I could tap at age fifty. Though a contributing factor to my early retirement, it did not prove decisive. Lacking the pension, I could have designed a more aggressive portfolio, as many of my club colleagues did. Wealth simply represents cash flow subjected to the catalyst of time and good money habits. As my story reveals, the catalyst works whether you come from humble beginnings or privilege.

Editor: *Well that seems hopeful! And I think maybe I do see a thematic thread in these meditations. Approach early retirement from a position of strength, and improve the world through inspirational projects.*

R. Beachley: Sounds good to me.

Editor: *And we can define an inspirational project as something we'd do for free?*

R. Beachley: Exactly. Think about your involvement with this project. I told you that you weren't likely to see any money from it. But look at all the fun you've had!

Editor: *Um, yeah. . .I kinda wanted to discuss that. . .But let me get us another round first. Peroni or Blue Moon?*

R. Beachley: Are you sure you can afford it?

Editor: *Afford it? Come on... what's ten or twelve dollars for a couple of beers between friends?*

R. Beachley: That couple of beers represents the annual dividend output of two hundred dollars invested at 6%. Is another round really worth jeopardizing two hundred dollars of permanent capital equivalence?

Editor: *please... go easy with this permanent capital equivalence stuff, OK? Do people really think like this?*

R. Beachley: They do if they're income investors!

About the Author

Over a twenty-year career as a communications director for the State of California, Rancroft Beachley helped produce reports, pamphlets, manuals, and brochures for various state entities, including the CSU system and CalPERS, where he worked with budget data, revenue data, actuarial projections, and regional economic forecasts. Alongside colleagues affiliated with Southern California chapters of the STC (Society for Technical Communication), he consulted in the production private industry technical publications. Having retired at fifty to pursue the *rentier* lifestyle, he resides in Los Angeles, maintains casual connection to former investment club members, and focuses on inspirational activities he happily does for free. He manages his portfolio according to the "balanced income" approach, generating annual yields in the 6% range, but considers an all-CEF portfolio a compelling idea in light of macroeconomic factors that support a lower-for-longer interest rate thesis. His rumored creative projects include an unfinished collection of income investing poetry, which he warns "will appeal only to discerning readers and generate only minor interest—pun intended."

PhantaSea Books

Honolulu, Hawaii

Phantasea Books publishes works of unique interest in a variety of genres, from adventure travel and historical fiction to subjects that transcend categories. Select titles include the following:

--*The Volcano Trilogy: A Philippines Surfing Odyssey*

(ISBN-13: 978-1450531801), an epic memoir of love and surfing in the Philippines. Reprinted in 2019 as an updated edition with additional photographs and postscript material, the narrative recounts how devotion to an island girl and commitment to a surf lifestyle enabled the author, Quinn Haber, to transform expat dreams into reality. Keen-eyed observations link descriptive detail to its social, historical, and cultural context and give readers a front-row seat to a locale few outsiders visit.

--*Islands on the Fringe: A Year of Micronesian Waves and Wanderers*

(ISBN-13: 978-06921922849), a wry portrayal of the ex-pat life, set in a lost latitude of the Pacific. From *Forward Reviews*: "S. Jacques Stratton's memoir is a bursting with life account of living on a tiny island. The cast is boisterous, animating the book with its charm. Stratton's Pacific is populated by Peace Corps workers, missionaries, and a vanishing breed of hardy adventurers who live off grid. They are captured in deft strokes and with gentle humor, as when a secretary—learning that Stratton, though from California, doesn't know Leonardo DiCaprio—scoffs, 'I know everyone from my village!'"

--Heart of a Traveler: Reflections from the Fathomless Edge of the World
(ISBN-13: 978-042832868), a thrilling anthology of travel adventure, short stories, and poetry based on the journeys of world traveler, surfer, seeker, and poet Ari Marsh. From the isolated, desert coastline of Baja California to high-altitude, hidden retreats in Northern India and beyond, the book presents us with a view of the world seldom seen, plunging us deep into the mysteries of life and into the depths of our own hearts.

--I Fell in Love with an Aleutian Vampire
(ISBN-13: 978-0578526997), a tale of love, war, and the power of faith. Relating the saga of Lieutenant Jake Harper, whose World War II assignment entailed a foray behind enemy lines into a realm of enduring twilight and even more enduring mystery, author Quinn Haber explores the difficulty of the Aleutian battle theatre, the native Aleuts and their vampire myths (the "*iidigidi*"), and the incredible journey of a US Army lieutenant sent there to fight.

--Old Lanai: A True Ghost Story from Hawaii
(ISBN- 13: 978-061578572), an excerpt from the journal of Warren S. Croft, a professor who traveled to Lanai in 1940 to investigate the disappearance of the villagers of Keomoku and subsequently disappeared himself, leaving behind only his journal and camera. "A true chiller of a tale from beginning to end" —*Midwest Book Review.*

--Echoes from the Sun: A Modern Quest for the Fountain of Youth (ISBN-13: 978-1466454897), a story rich with an array of fascinating international characters, chronicling the quest for truth and meaning that a young man embarks upon after discovering an ancient amulet hidden for centuries in the mountains of Baja California and believed to hold mysterious powers. A work that evokes *The Da Vinci Code* or the writing of Carlos Casteneda, *Echoes from the Sun* presents author Ari Marsh's exploration of the esoteric mysteries of life. "Remarkable! An astounding spiritual odyssey!"—*Randall Hayward, CEO/Founder, Taksu International*

--The Somali Pirate Trilogy, a tale of struggle at the intersection of subsistence living and international politics. In this three-part series comprised of *The Somali Pirate I* (ISBN-13: 978-1439239865), *Dagger Dogs of Zayid* (ISBN-13: 978-1460962244), and *White Star Empire* (ISBN-13: 978-0615669489), Quinn Haber presents the story of Noor Fayrus, whose introduction into the pirate life offers readers an unusual perspective on the complex issue of piracy near the Horn of Africa. "A political thriller and war fantasy dreamscape...offering insights about Somali culture, unconventional justifications for Somali piracy and just the right touch of fantasy"—*Kirkus Reviews*

--Tonkin (ISBN-13: 978-1439264140), a tale of high society, anarchists, and beasts set amid the 1889 Paris World Fair. Will dark forces and their terrible agenda detroy the Third Republic? Mystery, intrigue, and scenes from the golden age of Paris await in this work of genre fiction by Quinn Haber.

--*The Good Christian* (ISBN-13: 978-0578719139), a psychological thriller recounting how a young man's extreme acts of selflessness lead to an inspirational fate. Somewhere between the dark mind of a penitent and the radiant heart of a saint lies the soul of *The Good Christian* - a novella by Quinn Haber that will leave readers both horrified and inspired by one gentleman's extraordinary commitment to heavenly virtue in a world gone mad.

www.ingramcontent.com/pod-product-compliance
Lightning Source LLC
Chambersburg PA
CBHW031352040426
42444CB00005B/257